Science and
Spirituality:

*An Introduction for Students, Secular
People & the Generally Curious*

By Joseph J Berger

Science and Spirituality: An Introduction for Students, Secular People & the Generally Curious

Copyright © 2019 Onus Books

Published by *Onus Books*

Cover design: Onus Books

Trade paperback ISBN: 978-0-9935102-5-0

OB 15/25

Author's Note

In approximately 30 years as a college professor, I have taught biology, the scientific method and critical thinking to thousands of students. As students begin to understand the scientific worldview, they often have questions about how this relates to religion and spirituality in their lives. I found these conversations fascinating and I learned a lot from these intelligent and curious young people. It takes courage to question what you've long believed in the face of new knowledge. The willingness to be open to the possibility of changing your beliefs is a hallmark of scientific and critical thinking. The purpose of this work was to set down some of the knowledge and perspectives that these students found helpful. I hope that this will serve as the beginning of a fulfilling journey for many others as well.

Writing a book like this is a somewhat daunting task, from deciding what to include to having the audacity to even tackle the questions. There are many people over the years who have influenced and educated me. It would be impossible to list them all but some stand out for me.

I want to thank my wonderful family:
Dr. Deborah Fein, my wife, without whom this book wouldn't be. From early drafts to references, her intelligence, insight and confidence in me have been instrumental. For 38 years together, her intellect, kindness and infinite patience have kept me going.

My daughters Elizabeth and Emily, critical thinkers who even as children could point out flaws in my reasoning and keep me intellectually honest.

My brother Dan, a natural critical thinker and one of the sharpest minds I know.

Early in my education, I was strongly influenced by a teacher who set me on the right path as a scientist and teacher; Professor Steve Benson of Cal State East Bay. Thanks Steve.

My colleagues at Springfield College, who have been the source of many stimulating discussions:
Dr. Frank Torre
Rev. Bob Price
Dr. Rick Paar
David McMahon, Director of Spiritual Life at Springfield College, for supporting this work and for appreciating the spiritual aspect of secular people.

Thanks to the Freethinkers of the University of Connecticut, Storrs for helpful feedback.

I want to thank Kristin Wintermute, Director of Education at the American Humanist Association for valuable feedback about Humanism and the connected organizations.

I am especially grateful to Jonathan MS Pearce of Onus Books, author, philosopher, blogger and a great editor, for the insight, knowledge and patience he provided to this project.

Joseph Berger

Praise for the book:

Science and Spirituality is a refreshing introduction to the non-religious scientific worldview. Joseph Berger offers clarity to how religious and irreligious ideas do or do not entwine with science, making these complex topics accessible without opinion. This book is the perfect place to start in one's journey to better understand the role of religion and science in shaping our view of one another and the world.

Kristin Wintermute, Director of Education at the American Humanist Association.

*To my wife and partner, Deb, and to
our daughters, Elizabeth and Emily,
everything we could have hoped for.*

Science is not only compatible with spirituality; it is a profound source of spirituality. When we recognize our place in an immensity of light years and in the passage of ages, when we grasp the intricacy, beauty and subtlety of life, then that soaring feeling, that sense of elation and humility combined, is surely spiritual.

—Carl Sagan, from *The Demon-Haunted World*

Contents

Foreword

On a Need-to-Know Basis
By Ed Buckner, former President of American Atheists

Students (or the generally curious)—and that should in the best and broadest sense include all of us—need to know all sorts of things, some mundane and practical, some inspiring and enriching. All of us want, when we're eager to learn more about something, to be treated with respect and with an understanding that we need clear and honest information, including enough to give us an accurate grasp but without so much detail and background that it overwhelms us. All of us have at least some emotional investment in our religious or irreligious ideas, and we don't want our views to be attacked unnecessarily, even as we do want to learn more about other possibilities. When it comes to grappling with religion and science at the most basic, important levels, the right balance can be difficult to strike. Happily, Joseph Berger hits the mark squarely. He does not condescend or over-simplify, but he also does not ostentatiously show off his deep understanding just to impress us.

Even seasoned experts can be mistaken when they think they get it when it comes to what "spiritual" really means or what is and isn't a part of "the scientific method." The distinctions between science and technology can mislead even the wisest among us. The false notions that scientists or science are infallible or that truth automatically flows out of a lab may sometimes befuddle anyone. Whole libraries of books have been written about morality, evolution, secularism, cosmology, naturalism, DNA, critical thinking, progress, religiosity, atheism, and astronomy. In some sense, many of those books must be read to fully understand the details of those fields, but that is daunting. What we all need is to read something true and accurate but less daunting to get started. We need to know what we really must know first. Science and Spirituality is near perfect for that.

A book that defined all the key terms and outlined all the relevant facts could be so dry as to be unreadable, so dull as to be useless. The subjects included in this work are inherently interesting and so, happily if not inevitably, is the writing here. Wit and humor and introductions to fresh newer "gods" like The Flying Spaghetti Monster liven up the text. The reader is pulled along cheerfully on a fascinating voyage.

This short book provides a firm foundation for crucial intellectual development, allowing students (or secular people, or the merely curious) like you and me to gain serious understanding without demanding that we accept a particular viewpoint or political philosophy or religious or irreligious stance—and without demanding that we learn *everything* on any of the sub-subjects. Science infuses every aspect of our lives and culture, and misunderstanding what it is all about can make us miserable as well as ineffective. We need to know what education (not just schooling—education!) has to offer and what riches (mostly not financial, though those, too) can be ours. *Science and Spirituality* fills that niche with lively explanations and encouragement. This really is stuff we all need to know, presented in just the right way to be sure we'll learn.

Ed Buckner

Introduction

The first steps in a voyage of discovery

Whether you consider yourself to be secular, atheist, agnostic, spiritual but not religious, or you do consider yourself religious but are just curious about these non-religious ideas, this work will provide an introduction to the topic. Needless to say, a personal quest for meaning cannot be fulfilled by reading one source, so I will provide some ideas to think about, some science, and some references and links for further inquiry. Many of these are online references including Wikipedia. While Wikipedia is considered an "unstable" or even unreliable source by many, probably including some of your teachers, its accuracy is comparable to other encyclopedias and is useful for basic information, especially about science and for definitions of terms.[1,2] Wikipedia is also useful for the references and links to further information. Wikipedia is a "crowd-sourced" resource, with potential contributions by many people and some of these contributions are of better quality than others. But there are rules, and editors, and public comments and corrections. For this reason, poor information is often corrected quickly. In a sense Wikipedia is analogous to the way science itself works. In science there are rules and editors and reviewers, and contributions of varying quality. But science is self-correcting, even if it sometimes takes longer than Wikipedia. You must learn to be cautious about all information, and to seek confirmation and multiple sources.

I have personally checked the references I am providing and I consider them reliable as of the writing of this book. However, I am not going to provide links or references for every statement, and I encourage you to drill down into these ideas. Investigating ideas is part of the critical thinking journey I would encourage all my readers to embark upon. Please do not interpret any lack of a citation as implying a claim of originality on my part.

Because this work is intended as an introduction, I have deliberately kept it brief, to be accessible to an audience of students and other busy people. I know that you have coursework, reading assignments, a social life, and perhaps a job, and that you may not have time for a long book that you are not required to read. But there are many excellent works that expand on the ideas in this brief book, and I hope that after you get started here you will pursue those sources.

Use online resources; read some of the books that are mentioned here or that you discover in your searches; talk to friends and teachers. You have more education than most people throughout human history and readier access to information than anyone before the 21st century. This would be a good time to use them.

What is the difference between being secular and atheist or agnostic?

What does it mean to consider one's self to be secular? The simplest definition (from Meriam-Webster online) is "not religious." Similarly, Wikipedia describes it as "the state of being separate from religion...." But it's not that simple. Although many people who identify themselves as secular also consider themselves to be atheist (do not believe in the existence of God) or agnostic (they are not sure) the terms are not synonymous.

In 2017, the Public Religion Research Institute found that 24% of Americans are religiously unaffiliated (secular). This is larger than the number who belong to any single religious denomination. But only 27% of these secularists identify as atheist or agnostic. So not everyone who is unaffiliated with a religion is an atheist.[3]

What is an atheist?

Followers of the monotheistic Abrahamic religions, such as Christianity, Judaism or Islam profess a belief in a single "God." The idea of a single God has different names, Yahweh in the Jewish and Christian bibles, Allah in the Koran. Although these are different names for the same entity, these religions do have some differences in their concepts of what God is. I will use the word "god" with a lowercase "g" when referring to deities or the concept of deities in general, and "God" with a capital "G" when referring to the God of the monotheistic, or Abrahamic, religions.

An atheist, or non-theist, is a person who does not believe in the existence of a god or gods. Agnostic means "without knowledge," so an agnostic is someone who neither believes nor disbelieves in a god or gods, i.e. doesn't know. We can't know for sure how many gods people have believed in throughout human existence, but there are thousands of named gods in whom people currently or historically have believed. You can find the names of thousands of gods on the website godchecker.com, or on Wikipedia (see "Lists of deities"), so even the most devoutly religious monotheist is also a non-theist regarding several thousand other gods.

But if atheism is simply the absence of belief in a god, what does that mean for an atheist's ability to live a spiritual or moral life? Can one be secular and spiritual at the same time?

You may not believe in Zeus, but that does not affect your way of life. Similarly, atheism by itself is not a philosophy of life either. Atheism is a conclusion one comes to as a consequence of a particular worldview (scientific), but does not necessarily determine the way you live or your ability to be a spiritual or moral person.

Nonetheless, most people seek a philosophy of life or a way of looking at the world that helps us understand our place in the scheme of things and that provides insights into the big questions of life. Some of those questions now have scientific answers and others have provisional answers that are not scientifically demonstrated but are compatible with a scientific worldview. Whether you are not affiliated with a specific religion or you have concluded that there are no gods, you may still seek answers to the questions that have traditionally been the province of religion.

Secular *and* spiritual

A large and growing number of today's college students describe themselves as "secular." The 2013 American Religious Identification Survey of college students published by Trinity College in Connecticut[4] found that when college students were asked if they considered themselves to be religious, spiritual but not religious, or secular, 32% chose religious, 32% chose spiritual but not religious, and 28% chose secular. So, almost 2 out of 3 students say they are not religious. But a third say they are spiritual but not religious. How is it possible to be both secular and spiritual, or atheist and spiritual, or scientific and spiritual? At bottom, this is the question of how science and religion are compatible or incompatible, which I discuss below. First, we must define the scientific worldview.

The Scientific Worldview and Atheism

What does it mean to say that someone has a "scientific worldview"? What is the difference between "science" and a "scientific worldview"? Many people, especially students taking science classes, think of science as a collection of facts about the world, a body of knowledge. But science is a method as well as a body of knowledge, and the method is what leads to the knowledge. It might surprise you to learn that there is no universally agreed-upon definition of science, even among scientists.

Here are three definitions of science:

(1) "The use of evidence to construct testable explanations and predictions of natural phenomena, as well as the knowledge generated through this process."(National Academy of Sciences)[5]

(2) "…science is a way of knowing based on rational thought, skepticism, and evidence." (Biochemist Laurence Moran)[6]

(3) "Science is a way of thinking much more than it is a body of knowledge." (Astrophysicist Carl Sagan)

A scientific worldview is based on accepting the methods of

science as the most effective way of understanding the natural world. The scientific worldview is not just for scientists; it is a way of looking at the world that *at its core is based on evidence to support beliefs.*

A person who adopts a scientific worldview will be skeptical of beliefs based on insufficient evidence, including supernatural explanations, although they acknowledge that some things by their nature cannot have evidence. For example, if the world as you experience it is a computer-generated construct of your mind, referred to as the "simulation hypothesis" and depicted in the movie *The Matrix*, it would be difficult to find evidence to support or refute this.

Another viewpoint that also is not subject to evidence or proof is the belief that God created the universe at some point in the past, established the laws of nature and withdrew without any daily interference or miracles. This view (called Deism) gained popularity among Enlightenment intellectuals in the 18th century, and is seen by some as a transitional step to atheism. I think of it as "atheism light."

For more on the nature of evidence see the article in the Encyclopedia of Philosophy.[7]

Another term for the scientific worldview is *naturalism*. Strict, or strong, naturalism is called *metaphysical naturalism*. This is the belief that the <u>entire</u> universe is governed by consistent natural laws, and that all explanations for how the natural world works must be based on natural laws and natural phenomena.[8,9] In their work scientists are practicing *methodological naturalism*. This is the principle that the scientific method must be used to study the natural world and natural phenomena by reference to natural causes. Methodological naturalism is the basis for the spectacular success of science over at least four centuries in explaining the natural world. However, a scientist who practices methodological naturalism but does not rule out another realm that is independent of science, such as the existence of a god and miracles, is invoking the *supernatural*.[10] If such a scientist resorts to supernatural explanations for any aspect of their work, this undermines confidence in a scientific explanation and a scientific understanding of the phenomenon.

A Pew survey in 2009 found that only 33% of scientists surveyed believed in God. Another 14% said they believed in a "higher power or universal spirit."[11] In 1998 a study published in Nature[12] found that 93% of "elite scientists," defined as members of the National Academy of Sciences, did not believe in a personal god, a god who has an identity and consciousness, and who can hear and answer prayers;[10] 77% did not believe in personal immortality.[13] Results vary of course, depending on who was asked and what questions were asked, but it's safe to say that most scientists don't believe in God. This follows from the fact that most scientists have a scientific worldview, and find that the evidence for the existence of a god is lacking.

The Scientific Worldview and Religion

This leads to the issue of the relationship between science (or the scientific worldview) and religion. The subject of whether science and religion are compatible, that is whether you can have a scientific worldview and simultaneously hold religious beliefs, is

9

a topic of much debate among scientists and philosophers. The late biologist Stephen Jay Gould suggested that science and religion deal with "non-overlapping magisteria" (NOMA);[14] in other words, they study different realms of knowledge that do not have anything to say about one another. Many scientists disagree. For example, the evolutionary biologist Richard Dawkins has written that since supernatural events claimed by religion, such as miracles or the power of prayer, would, in fact, leave evidence, then it is reasonable to demand such evidence.[15] These two main viewpoints among scientists are usually referred to as accommodationist (science and religion are compatible, they accommodate each other) and anti-accommodationist (they are not compatible). A metaphysical naturalist would conclude that they are not, while a methodological naturalist might conclude that they are, or might not (but they assume naturalism for trying to work out what is actually going on in the world around them).

However, even strong metaphysical naturalists, while rejecting supernatural explanations, certainly do ponder spiritual questions. What is "spirituality" to a naturalist? Once again, there is much debate over this word. Many naturalists and atheists reject the word "spiritual" as implying something supernatural, involving ghosts or invisible spirits. But that is only one definition of spiritual, and as Sam Harris explains,[16] there are meanings of "spiritual" that are quite compatible with a scientific worldview. The quote by Carl Sagan from *"The Demon-Haunted World"* at the beginning of this chapter is an example.[17] In *"The God Delusion,"* Richard Dawkins refers to himself as "a deeply religious non-believer."[18] This emphasizes the compatibility between a non-theistic, scientific worldview and a spiritual sense of wonder at nature. Many other people have found the scientific worldview to be spiritually satisfying, among them the astrophysicist Neil deGrasse Tyson, the late writer Christopher Hitchens, and even Albert Einstein and Charles Darwin.

According to Pew Research,[19] not all atheists see a contradiction between atheism and spiritual pondering about their place in the world. About a third [of atheists] say they feel a deep sense of spiritual peace and often think about the meaning and purpose of life. Half report that they feel a deep sense of wonder about the universe and a majority feel a deep connection with nature and the earth. As Douglas Adams wrote in The Hitchhiker's Guide to the Galaxy, "Isn't it enough to see that a garden is beautiful without having to believe that there are fairies at the bottom of it too?"

One definition of spirituality that is consistent with a strong naturalistic worldview can be found in the principles of World Pantheism: "By spirituality and spiritual we don't mean any kind of supernatural or non-physical activity. We mean our deeper emotions and aesthetic responses towards Nature and the wider Universe—our sense of our place in these, and the ethics and values that these feelings imply."[20]

So while not all naturalists agree on the exact definition of spirituality, most seem to believe that a scientific understanding of the natural world, such as the origins and vast scale of the universe and the basis and interconnectedness of life serve to help us appreciate our place in the greater scheme of existence and can help guide our understanding of how to live one's life.

11

Many people have already come to the conclusion that an ancient system of belief, created before modern science existed, is no longer adequate to explain the physical world or to help us solve the problems that may threaten our very existence. Perhaps you also find religious explanations of the world to be unsatisfying or inadequate to inform your spiritual perspective. Maybe you are just beginning to think about it. In either case, you probably have some questions.

What about the Big Questions?

Science can certainly help to answer some of the big questions, like how the universe began or how humans came to be. But can it help answer other questions about existence and the search for meaning that religion has traditionally sought to answer? What happens when you die; is there life after death; is there reincarnation? How do we know right from wrong if we don't rely on ancient writings like the Bible or modern works by religious leaders? What is our place in the world? Is there a purpose to human existence? Can science provide the sense of mystery and awe that many people find in religion? What spiritual satisfaction is available if I choose a reality-based, naturalistic, worldview?

Project2061 of the American Association for the Advancement of Science (AAAS) makes the point that science is not able to provide complete answers to all questions:

> There are many matters that cannot usefully be examined in a scientific way. There are, for instance, beliefs that—by their very nature—cannot be proved or disproved (such as the

existence of supernatural powers and beings, or the true purposes of life). In other cases, a scientific approach that may be valid is likely to be rejected as irrelevant by people who hold to certain beliefs (such as in miracles, fortune-telling, astrology, and superstitions). Nor do scientists have the means to settle issues concerning good and evil although they can sometimes contribute to the discussion of such issues by identifying the likely consequences of particular actions, which may be helpful in weighing alternatives.[21]

Certainly, some questions are beyond the scope of science, especially if you are seeking 100% certainty. But there are perspectives on these major questions that are consistent with science and can still be spiritually satisfying. I will provide some brief answers to the questions that science does address, and present some perspectives on the less concrete questions for you to consider, discuss and investigate further. Part of the enjoyment of a rational worldview is to work out some of the answers for ourselves. For example, can we find our own meaning in life? We will return to that question later.

Part I—Why science?

Religion is a system of wishful illusions together with a disavowal of reality, such as we find nowhere else but in a state of blissful hallucinatory confusion. Religion's eleventh commandment is 'Thou shalt not question.'

—Sigmund Freud

The good thing about science is that it's true whether or not you believe in it.

—Neil deGrasse Tyson

Science as a problem solver

Science is based on the idea that there is an objective, actual reality, which is independent of artificial, human, cultural reality (i.e., what we are taught to believe). Science's reality is sometimes called "nature" or "the natural world." Science is a method for ascertaining information about that objective reality that takes into account the ways in which human perceptions and beliefs can be deceived, and it attempts to correct for the shortcomings of the human brain, including distortions introduced by human culture. It is not perfect, nor is it free of abuses since it is employed by fallible humans. But one of the fundamental aspects of science is that it is self-correcting.

Everything about science is subject to modification, revision, and improvement. The facts discovered by science are considered provisional and are constantly changing. Even the methods of science are subject to constant modification and improvement. Scientists understand that any scientific explanation is only the best version we have based on current knowledge, and it can change. In science that's a feature, not a bug. It allows science to continually improve its explanatory concepts. This uncertainty inherent in the scientific method often seems unsatisfying to many people, who tend to want definite answers, not uncertainties.

Another principle of science related to the inherent uncertainty in our knowledge is exemplified in the quote attributed to the ancient Greek playwright Euripides, "Question everything" (also see Freud's quote above). Important contributions to our understanding of the natural world go back at least to the ancient Greeks, but the modern scientific era began in the 17th century when people began to question ancient knowledge about the world in such areas as astronomy, chemistry and physiology. This led to discoveries that stood up to repeated testing and examination, and a Scientific Revolution. Science is by far the best system we currently have for learning about the natural world and for testing solutions to problems.

Here is possibly the most dramatic evidence for the value of science: Until around 1800, through all the centuries when a pre-scientific worldview prevailed, the average human life expectancy was about 35 years of age, with half of all children dying before the age of 15. This average reflects disease, infection, death in childbirth and untreatable traumas. Life expectancy began to rise with the Scientific Revolution, and since 1900 the average life expectancy has roughly doubled. So, in a real sense, science has given everyone in the developed world *two lifetimes*, (on average) an accomplishment unequalled by any other worldview or non-scientific interpretation of reality.

One consequence of this is that the population of the world has increased dramatically, and we face serious problems related to this increased population. The grandparents of the students entering college today were born into a world of two billion people. It now contains over seven billion, and by 2050 there will probably be around nine billion. All these people will need safe food, clean water, shelter, energy, health care and education, while preventing catastrophic climate change, epidemic disease and global conflict. Solving these problems requires genuine critical thinking. If we fail, there is a good chance that our species could cease to exist.

Assuming that a solution is possible, we must take a path that leads to a workable solution before we become extinct. If one group believes they have the right answer and they impose it on the rest of the world without allowing questioning and testing, and it turns out not to be the right solution, then humans could be finished as a species. But we know science works well, and has the best chance of being the most successful path to a solution. We must use science to find the answers. Too long a delay down the wrong path, or worse, taking a path from which it is impossible to recover, can make all the difference. We do not have time for random trial and error.

A religious worldview could cause a potentially fatal delay because it can lead people to relinquish responsibility to a higher force. It implies that God will provide, or will present us with a solution to the problem, or that whatever happens is up to God and not to us. We must avoid resorting to God and religion as a viable choice for the way to save our species because it will almost certainly prevent us from finding the right answers in time.

Why is science a better approach than faith-based solutions? Science uses strict tests of reality based on evidence, while faith makes a virtue of uncritical thinking. Science never asks you to accept anything on faith and always provides evidence for any claims. The practical and urgent problems we are facing need practical solutions, to which religion has little to contribute. But science can address all of them, if given a chance.

Accepting that science is the problem-solving path most likely to succeed can be compatible with *methodological* naturalism, but most scientists are *metaphysical* naturalists. That is, they don't just believe in the scientific method for advancing knowledge, but believe that the natural world is all there is.

Why science rejects faith

Faith is believing something you know ain't true.

—Mark Twain

If someone is a methodological naturalist, they may embrace the scientific method as the best way to gain new information, while holding a belief in the supernatural. The weakness in this approach comes from the requirement that you must hold two different, contradictory worldviews. In scientific research aimed at answering questions about the natural world, such a person must use a strict evidence-based standard. But at the same time, they may also subscribe to the belief that there are supernatural phenomena for which there is no evidence. For example, a miracle, defined in the Oxford online dictionary as an "...event that is not explicable by natural or scientific laws and is therefore considered to be the work of a divine agency."[22] Compare this to the same dictionary's definition of magic: "...influencing the course of events by using mysterious or supernatural forces." In other words, a purely methodological naturalist must believe in the value of evidence while at the same time believing in magic, positions that most scientists find incompatible.

Once you decide that science has the best chance of solving our practical problems, you may begin to find it difficult to accept other assertions on faith. For example, belief in the existence of God, who is essentially an invisible sky magician who can read your mind, grant wishes, make you live longer, redirect the tornado away from your house or make your football team win, and for which there is absolutely no evidence, may seem outdated or childish to some people. But rejecting faith and accepting a scientific worldview can be a very difficult process, especially if you were raised with strong religious teachings. You must be willing to use your powers of reasoning and think for yourself. You must try to get past what your parents and community taught you and what peer pressure from your community may be imposing on you, including the intense resistance that often comes from "people of faith" whose beliefs are challenged. The religious frequently regard atheists as among the most reviled groups. A survey by the Public Religion Research Institute found that public support for businesses to refuse service to someone based on their religious belief has increased significantly since 2014.[23] Nearly one in four Americans say small businesses should be allowed to refuse to serve atheists if doing so is against their religious beliefs. Don't let that discourage you. Many marginalized groups have been and are being discriminated against, some much more viciously than atheists. But progress has been made in recent years due to brave people who were willing to fight for justice.

The next chapter considers the scientific answers to questions traditionally addressed by religion.

Part II—Answers in Science

The Natural World

Religion has existed since long before recorded history. There is archaeological evidence of burial rituals that indicate a belief in an afterlife going back as much as 100,000 years. Religion served to explain natural phenomena, such as day and night, seasons, the weather, as well as disease and death. Most people today accept the scientific explanations for natural phenomena and no longer view angry gods or evil spirits as the source of disease, bad weather or failed crops, but this is not true of everyone. In 2010, a poll found that 55 percent of people in sub-Saharan Africa believe in witchcraft, usually as the cause of disease or misfortune.[24] It is reported that, between 2000 and 2012, at least 2100 people were killed in India after being accused of witchcraft.[25] There are many references to witches and witchcraft in the Bible, and many people in Western society also believe in witchcraft and demons. In July 2014, Pope Francis gave official Church recognition to an organization of Catholic priests who conduct exorcisms. Some Christian parents forbid their children to read the Harry Potter books because they depict witches and wizards as heroes. Clearly, we are far from everyone accepting strictly natural explanations for natural phenomena.

The main function of science is to explain the natural world. Some scientific explanations are now so widely accepted by educated people—for example, that the Earth revolves around the sun, not the other way around; weather can be explained (and sometimes predicted) by meteorology; the Earth is not the center of the universe—that it is not necessary to go into them here. However, there are some scientific explanations for natural phenomena that are not widely known by people who have not studied science and which had previously been explained by religion. So, I will try briefly to explain some of them. These explanations are based on what we know so far, but they will likely change as we get better information.

Where Did We Come From?

The Universe

The study of the origins, physical laws and possible fate of the universe from a naturalistic perspective is called physical cosmology. Many of the answers that cosmology provides are still provisional, but we have a fairly solid basis for what follows.

In the beginning, there was nothing. The Big Bang was the moment approximately 13.7 billion years ago in which a minute singularity (a point with no dimensions), smaller than an atom, expanded very rapidly to form energy, matter and time. The first matter consisted of elementary particles, smaller than atoms. They coalesced into protons, neutrons and electrons, held together by other subatomic particles. All the matter of the early universe was hydrogen and helium. (Hydrogen consists of a single proton in the nucleus with one electron in orbit around it. Helium, the next simplest atom, is a nucleus of two protons and two neutrons with two electrons orbiting the nucleus.) Even today the mass of the visible universe is about 75% hydrogen and 24% helium. We don't know how large the universe is, but the edge of the "visible" universe is about 46 billion light-years away.[26] (A light-year is the distance light can travel in a year—about 6 trillion miles.) The "visible" universe refers to the farthest that light could have travelled to us since the beginning of the universe.

Mass has gravity, and gravitational attraction led to the formation of huge objects made of hydrogen and helium. When their mass becomes large enough, the enormous gravity of these objects smashes the simpler atomic nuclei together through nuclear fusion, and a star is born. Nuclear fusion releases large amounts of energy and results in the heat, light and radiation of stars. When the fusion process forces simple atomic nuclei together into larger aggregates of protons and neutrons, new elements heavier than hydrogen and helium are formed in these stars. Eventually, the stars come to the end of their life cycle and explode; thus, the heavier elements formed in the stars are released into space. These coalesce into newer stars with heavier elements in them and nuclear fusion starts again. The current scientific understanding is that all elements heavier than hydrogen and helium were formed inside stars. Thus the essential elements of life, including carbon, nitrogen, oxygen, phosphorus as well as metals like iron and calcium were formed inside stars. As the astronomer Carl Sagan famously said, we are all made of star-stuff.

Our Solar System

Our sun and its planets and other objects formed about 4.5 billion years ago from material that included elements that had already been through the life cycle of one or more stars. Our solar system is located in an outer arm of what we call the Milky Way galaxy,

23

about 30,000 light-years from the center of the galaxy. There are about one hundred billion stars in the Milky Way, and as of 2019, it is estimated that there are as many as two trillion galaxies in the known universe. When you look up at the night sky many of the points of light that appear to be single stars are actually entire galaxies far from the Milky Way.

Our planet, Earth, exists at a distance from the Sun that results in a surface temperature that allows water to exist in a liquid form. This is crucial to the existence of life, as we know it. Sometimes this ideal distance from the sun is referred to as the "Goldilocks Zone" because it is not too hot or too cold, but is just right.

Some individuals have suggested that the Goldilocks Zone, and our place in it, is evidence for the existence of God. But consider—if there are trillions of planets and only a small percent fulfill the Goldilocks conditions, there would still be many planets capable of supporting life.

Life on Earth

This is a simplified explanation from a biologist.

Life on Earth is a carbon-based system of self-replicating entities (organisms), which use the molecule DNA to store the instructions for metabolism and reproduction. The smallest unit of life is a cell, meaning all living things are made of one or more cells. Cells can carry out the functions of metabolism and reproduction using the instructions contained in DNA. The basic structure of DNA and the code contained within it is essentially the same for all life on Earth, indicating that life on Earth has a common origin. We sometimes call this the "unity of life."

We know approximately when life on Earth began: at least 3.5-3.8 billion years ago, based on existing physical evidence. *How* life began is the subject of much scientific interest and hypothesis, but is not known with any degree of certainty. One hypothesis that is gaining acceptance is that it began at the bottom of oceans using the energy and materials found at hydrothermal vents.[27] What we do know is that, once life began, it changed and morphed into the diversity we see today through the process of evolution.

When a system possesses properties that are more complex than just the sum of its parts, we call that an "emergent property." Life is, therefore, an emergent property of matter and energy that are organized in a particular way. The atoms that constitute a living organism are no different from the atoms of non-living matter. It is their organization, under the direction of DNA, and the use of energy to keep them organized that distinguishes living from non-living matter.

As far as we can determine, the life that exists on Earth today only began once (because of the "unity of life" principle). If there were other origins of life their descendants do not exist today, and they have left no evidence that has yet been discovered. One interesting property of DNA-based life that has allowed it to evolve and adapt so well on Earth is that the DNA copying process makes just the *right amount of mistakes*. These mistakes are called mutations, which are explained later in this section. If there were not enough mistakes there would be no changes and therefore no adaptation to new conditions; too many mistakes and the benefits of useful mutations would disappear over time.

No one has yet figured out how to create life in the laboratory. DNA is still the only repository of the "knowledge" of how to use energy to organize matter into an arrangement that is alive. You could say that DNA contains the "secret" of how to make life, which has been passed on in an unbroken chain since life began.

Living things, organisms, are basically organized piles of molecules. What keeps the molecules organized into a system capable of metabolism and reproduction is the use of energy. All matter will move from a more organized state to a more random state, in a process called entropy, unless energy is used to keep the system organized and functional. So, life requires matter, energy and instructions.

Metabolism is a process whereby energy is used to keep these molecules organized. All living things need to use energy in this way. Plants can capture energy directly from the sun through photosynthesis; plants and organisms that can capture energy directly are called autotrophs (which means they make their own food). Autotrophs then store the energy in the chemical bonds of molecules. All living things that do not capture energy directly, called heterotrophs, must acquire energy that is stored in the chemical bonds of complex molecules, which we call food. Food also provides matter, the molecular building blocks necessary to construct organisms. It is important to note that all the food of heterotrophs comes from living things. There is no heterotroph that does not require molecules from other living things as its food source. (Even plants obtain some of their matter from other living things.) In other words, no living thing can exist in isolation but instead they depend on an intricate, interdependent web of life to survive.

Here are more details about that process. It starts when plants use energy from sunlight to combine simpler molecules like carbon dioxide and water, plus minerals like nitrogen and phosphorous, into larger molecules like sugars, proteins and fats. These larger, complex molecules store some of the energy within their chemical bonds. Other organisms eat the plants, and the molecules with the stored energy (food) are passed from one organism to another in a form that can be used by living things.

The stored energy is used to make and break other chemical bonds, so the matter is formed and reformed as it moves through the chain of life. At each step, the total amount of stored energy is reduced. Eventually, the matter ends up as carbon dioxide, water and minerals again and the energy becomes random heat (entropy again). Energy from the sun can then be used to reform the complex molecules, and the cycle repeats.

Therefore, all life on Earth is connected through the following:

1- its common origin.
2- its possession of the common DNA code that holds the instructions for how to "make" life.
3- its necessity to sustain life by consuming living things (plants, animals) or the products of living things (fruit, eggs, milk), in essence, "life" moving in and out of other living things.
4- its interdependence through the matter/energy web of

life.

5- its ultimate reliance on the sun for the energy to sustain life.

Since its origin on Earth, life has expanded and morphed into the complex interdependent system we see today. Carbon-based cellular life using DNA for instructions has been very successful on Earth. It is the only life form and it has expanded to occupy virtually every niche on Earth. (Ecologically speaking, a niche is a way to "make a living" as an organism.) The process through which the original life on Earth became the millions of species we now see is explained by the Theory of Evolution. This explanation was first proposed by Charles Darwin and Alfred Russell Wallace in the 1850s, and since then has been refined and confirmed by many people through extensive experimentation and observation. It explains both the unity of life and the diversity of life. Evolution also explains where humans came from, who and what we are, what our place is in the natural world on Earth and gives clues as to where we might be heading.

Evolution

It is important to distinguish the *fact that evolution has happened* from the ideas about *how it happens*. There is no disagreement among scientists, or among most educated people, that evolution has happened. There is still interesting debate about some of the details of how it has happened. Evolution is the process whereby life on Earth has changed over time; there is no disagreement among scientists that this has occurred. Species exist today that did not exist in the past, and species existed in the past that do not exist today. The most direct evidence for this comes from the fossil record. In Darwin's time, people were just starting to understand that fossils were the remains of types of animals and plants that no longer exist.

The Theory of Evolution is the *idea* of how evolution works; it is an explanation of the basic mechanisms of evolution. In science, a theory is a very well supported explanation with extensive evidence to back it up. It's not the same as the general use of the word theory to mean a good guess that is untested. Scientists would call that a hypothesis.

Many people are surprised to learn that the Theory of Evolution is actually rather simple and is based on ideas that most people today readily accept as true. When Charles Darwin proposed it in 1859,[28] much of the scientific evidence was relatively new, such as the significance of fossils, or was still undiscovered, such as the basis for genetic inheritance. The following list contains the basic components of Darwin's theory. If you read this list and think about each item you will likely find that there is not any statement that you believe to be false or that is not generally considered a fact, yet in Darwin's time, every one of these was controversial. Since then, over 150 years of scientific testing has confirmed each of these parts of Darwin's theory.

1- More individuals (plants, animals, people) are born than can possibly survive to reproduce.
2- No two individuals in a sexually-reproducing population are exactly alike.
3- Some of those differences may provide an advantage (stronger, faster, etc.).
4- Since not all individuals can survive, some of those who

survive may do so because of these advantageous traits ("natural selection").

5- Those that survive will pass those advantageous traits ("adaptations") on to their offspring (inheritance).

6- Darwin proposed that there must be some way that small changes to the means of inheritance get introduced over time (now called mutations).

7- People have been doing something similar, selecting the most desirable animals and plants, for thousands of years to produce domesticated animals and plants (selective breeding or "artificial selection").

8- The Earth is many millions of years old, not just 6000 years old as the Bible says, so there has been time for natural selection to work to produce the variety of life we now see. (We now know it's actually *billions* of years old, which makes an even stronger case.)

Pretty simple, right? If you think all these points are true, then you understand the Theory of Evolution.

Human Evolution

Where did human beings come from? Human beings arose, like all species on Earth, through the process of evolution. Through survival, reproduction, and small changes in the DNA instructions (caused by mutations), combined with various conditions in the environment that favored certain mutations (natural selection), our species appeared about 200,000 years ago. Prior to (and after) that, there were other species of human-like creatures, but there are no examples of them alive today. The sole surviving species is called *Homo sapiens sapiens*, or modern humans: us.

If humans came from apes why are there still apes?

Homo sapiens, as well as the other extinct human-like species, evolved from a common ancestor with apes that lived about 6 million years ago. An important point to understand is that apes, such as chimpanzees and humans, *share* a common ancestor. Humans did not evolve *from* modern apes or *from* chimps. And since both modern humans and modern apes are all the result of 6 million years of evolution since the common ancestor, humans are not "more evolved" than apes. We are just different. An analogy can be seen in the British and the Americans. America is an English-speaking country with many cultural similarities to Britain. We know that America started as an offshoot of Britain. Yet both America and Britain today are quite different from Britain of the eighteenth century. And you don't hear people saying, "If America came from Britain why are there still British people?"

Is there a direction to evolution?

Biologists often point out that there is no "direction" to evolution. Evolution occurs based on a combination of random events, such as genetic mutations and changes in the environment, and non-random natural selection. Evolution is a continuous process, which has no goal or any way of predicting or planning for the future. However, in hindsight, it may be possible to see a sort of "theme" in evolution: The evolution of life on Earth can be viewed as a progression of increasing levels of cooperation. From the partnership between two kinds of bacteria that led to complex cells about 2 billion years ago,[29] to groups of cells cooperating to create multicellular life less than 1

31

billion years ago, even to the growth of human society from family bands to modern civilizations, cooperation has often been the key to a leap in evolutionary success. The idea that when people cooperate, instead of only competing, everyone benefits is sometimes referred to as a non-zero-sum game (i.e., that the gains and losses of the interaction do not cancel each other out),[30] also known as a win-win situation.

Causes of disease

For most of human history, disease was thought to be the result of witchcraft, demonic possession or punishment from the gods. The scientific explanation is that some diseases are caused by infections, some are inherited, some are the result of nutritional deficiencies and some causes are still unknown. Although most people today understand this, it might be useful to summarize it here.

In the mid-1500s the idea was proposed that tiny invisible particles of some kind were responsible for infectious disease. Over the next centuries, observation and experimentation led to the acceptance of the Germ Theory of Disease in the late 1800s, the explanation that infectious disease is caused by microorganisms such as bacteria and viruses. This took several hundred years after the invention of the microscope because there was a lot of observation and experimentation necessary. An understanding of the role of germs in causing disease is the foundation for vaccination, water and sewage sanitation, refrigeration of food, pasteurization of milk, disinfection and sterile techniques in medicine. Antibiotics, discovered in the late 1920s, are effective against bacteria but do not affect viral infections. The Germ Theory may be more responsible for the increase in human life expectancy since the late 1800s than any other scientific idea.

In 1953 Watson and Crick described the structure of DNA[31] (the molecule of heredity) and this has led to a growing understanding of the genetic basis of inherited, non-infectious, diseases. Routine correction of genetic diseases has not been achieved yet, but it is scientifically plausible. Great progress has been made in this area, though much work remains to be done.

Cancer has multiple causes: some inherited, some due to viruses, and some due to DNA damage from various sources including environmental chemicals and ionizing radiation such as x-rays, cosmic rays and ultraviolet from sunlight. There is no reliable evidence that electromagnetic radiation that is non-ionizing, such as from cell phones, causes cancer. Microwave ovens cook food using short-wavelength radio waves, not nuclear radiation. No sort of ionizing radiation is left in the food after cooking, any more than the walls of a room continue to glow after you turn off the lights.

Miracles

People often use the word "miracle" to describe either an event of low probability, such as surviving a disaster or something that evokes wonder, such as the birth of a baby. But people also use the word to mean something that defies natural law, presumably through the agency of a supernatural being, such as a miracle attributed to God. Another name for that is magic. If you subscribe to a naturalistic worldview, natural processes can explain all natural phenomena. Just because we don't currently know the explanation does not mean it is magic. There are no documented examples of "miracles" that stand up to close examination. Joe Nickell is a prominent investigator of miracle claims, and his book *The Science of Miracles: Investigating the Incredible* is a fascinating description of his investigations of reported miracles.

Prayer

Some prayer is a petition for something and is based on the presumption of communication with God and that God might grant these wishes. Prayer that petitions God to intervene to grant wishes on behalf of someone else is called intercessory prayer (IP). This is not compatible with naturalism. There is no evidence that prayers result in desired outcomes more often than chance. A meta-analysis (study of studies) in 2006 concluded that "There is no scientifically discernable effect for IP as assessed in controlled studies."[32,33]

However, there is also prayer of the kind that would be considered contemplative, or meditative, which is not an appeal for magic favors. That is different and is compatible with naturalism.

Part III—Morality

The greatest tragedy in mankind's entire history may be the hijacking of morality by religion.

—Arthur C. Clark

Does our sense of right and wrong come from religion?

Many people assert that our sense of morality comes from religious teachings and that if we were all atheists there would be nothing to stop us from killing, robbing and raping with impunity. If a person presents that argument, a reasonable question would be to ask them if they were to find out today that there was absolutely no God, would they then go out and commit those crimes? We have a moral sense that does not depend on fear of punishment in the afterlife, and is enforced by the law. The illusionist and atheist Penn Jillette has said, "The question I get asked by religious people all the time is, without God, what's to stop me from raping all I want? And my answer is: I do rape all I want. And the amount I want is zero. And I do murder all I want, and the amount I want is zero. The fact that these people think that if they didn't have this person watching over them that they would go on killing, raping rampages is the most self-damning thing I can imagine." In other words, acting in a "moral" way only because of fear of punishment is a childish form of morality. Civilized adults do not need the fear of punishment to know right from wrong.

In fact, the Bible is filled with commands to commit acts of murder and genocide in the name of God, which we consider immoral or criminal today. For example, Moses commands the

35

Israelites to exterminate the tribe of Midian (Numbers 31:7-18 King James Version). Scripture also instructs us to kill witches: "Thou shalt not suffer a witch to live" (Exodus 22:18), and "A man also or woman that hath a familiar spirit, or that is a wizard, shall surely be put to death: they shall stone them with stones" (Leviticus 20:27) and to kill homosexuals: "If a man also lie with mankind, as he lieth with a woman, both of them have committed an abomination: they shall surely be put to death" (Leviticus 20:13); and to kill our children if they talk back: "For every one that curseth his father or his mother shall be surely put to death" (Leviticus 20:9).

If the Bible is actually the revealed word of an all-powerful, all-knowing God rather than a collection of writings by human beings who lived a very long time ago, why does it not contain any information that was not known 2500 years ago? Why not "Thou shalt not kill old women for witchcraft; there are no witches"? Or how about a hint that the cause of infectious disease is tiny life forms too small to see? Why does it forbid the mixing of linen and wool in the same garment (Leviticus 19:19), but fails to forbid the mixing of sewage and drinking water, which would have saved humanity a lot of grief, not to mention hundreds of millions of deaths over the several millennia that it took to figure it out for ourselves? If believers answer that God wants us to figure it out for ourselves, then why did he not want us to figure out the other discoveries of science, such as evolution? Why all the advice about how to treat slaves, instead of forbidding slavery? The Bible was codifying the morality of that period and place in history, and much of what was then considered moral is now viewed by us with horror.

These are only a few examples of the ways in which we do not, in fact, derive many of our modern moral values from ancient scriptures. For more on this, see *God is Not Great* by Christopher Hitchens, *The God Delusion* by Richard Dawkins, and *The End of Faith* by Sam Harris. These books are highly recommended for further reading about the failures of traditional religion to inform what we currently view as moral ways of living.

History is full of examples of mass murder, inquisitions and genocides committed in the name of religion, and official organized religion is hardly a source of reliable moral guidance. In March of 2009, the BBC reported that the Catholic Church excommunicated a doctor in Brazil for performing an abortion to save the life of a 9-year-old girl who was pregnant with twins after being raped by her stepfather.[34] As Sam Harris points out in *The Moral Landscape*, the Catholic Church "did not excommunicate a single member of the Third Reich for committing genocide."[35]

The modern origins of the philosophical position that morality is determined by human beings and does not derive from the revealed word of God can be seen in the writings of the Dutch Renaissance philosopher Baruch Spinoza.[36] His work is considered a foundation of the Enlightenment. The philosophy he developed is called Pantheism. It is the idea that there is no supernatural God, only the natural world, and that "God" is the entirety of nature and the universe.

In fact, our collective sense of right and wrong has changed substantially over time, not only in the past 2500 years but even in the last few hundred years. In the Middle Ages, the public torture and burning of cats was considered entertainment;[37] today it would be considered pathological and abhorrent behavior. Human prisoners were tortured, dismembered and brutally executed as public entertainment, often for religious transgressions. Today, even most people who support the death penalty are horrified by reports of prisoners who appear to have suffered during execution. Rather than derive our modern moral standards from religious writings, human societies (generally) have evolved a more humane sense of ethics independent of religious teachings. Though some people have claimed that this evolution comes from religious teachings, it is in fact religion that has changed (and sometimes lagged) to match our modern sense of right and wrong.

You may sometimes hear religious people argue that Hitler, Stalin and Mao, who collectively were responsible for as many as 100 million deaths, were atheists, and therefore atheism equals mass murder and genocide. There are several problems with this argument. First, Hitler was not an atheist; the Third Reich persecuted atheists. Hitler was a Catholic and professed his belief in a Christian God numerous times in his speeches, and Nazi military uniform hardware carried the phrase "Gott mit uns" (God is with us). Hitler worked with the cooperation of the Catholic Church and was never excommunicated. After World War II the Vatican issued passports and visas to help some Nazi war criminals escape prosecution.[38,39,40]

Second, it is unclear the extent to which the other mass murderers may have been atheists, but even if they were, this is irrelevant. Hitler, Stalin and Genghis Khan all had mustaches, but it is highly unlikely that mustaches cause mass murder. Remember, atheism is not a complete worldview or philosophy. It is merely the absence of belief in a magical god. If all the above-named killers did not believe in the Tooth Fairy, does that mean that not believing in the Tooth Fairy causes one to commit to mass murder? It would require some rather convoluted philosophical reasoning to link mass murder with not believing in God.

So, if we have a scientific worldview, how can we determine the right way to behave toward our fellow humans? For one, the scientific understanding of how nervous systems work, what causes pain, and what is necessary to achieve physical wellbeing can inform our decisions about right and wrong. In the Middle Ages, animals were thought not to feel pain since they did not possess "souls," which made torture for entertainment morally acceptable. We now know that all mammalian nervous systems are very similar, and we do not condone or even allow the torture or mistreatment of sentient (feeling) animals. Most people today would even find it repulsive and pathological to find a child torturing flies or ants for fun. Part of the reason for this is that our scientific understanding of the biology of sensation has influenced our sense of morality.

Studies also suggest that people even in different cultures have a similar concept of important aspects of right and wrong, such as fairness and justice. A current topic of great interest in cognitive science is the question of whether humans are born with a sense of right and wrong, and whether there is an evolutionary explanation for this. This concept is called Universal Moral Grammar (UMG) and is the subject of much research. A paper by John Mikhail in 2007 described the theory and the then-current evidence that strongly suggested that people do in fact have an inborn morality. This can be seen in small children, in people of different cultures, and in atheists just as much as in religious people.[41] For example, there is a moral dilemma commonly called the Trolley Problem. The question is posed: If a trolley is about to run over and kill five people working on a train track, and you have the ability to switch the trolley onto a side track where it will kill one person and save the five, is it morally acceptable to do this? Most people say yes. But if five people need five different organ transplants to save their lives, is it morally acceptable to grab a healthy person and kill them to harvest their organs? Most people say no. Morality isn't just rational philosophy—it also involves emotion, such as empathy. In fact, there is credible evidence for rudimentary concepts of fairness and justice and other building blocks of morality in animals, linking moral behavior to evolution.[42]

The idea of an evolutionary explanation for a universal human moral sense was also expressed in Robert Wright's 1994 book, *The Moral Animal*.

A 2010 book by Sam Harris (*The Moral Landscape*) makes the case that we can use science to build a moral code. Needless to say, not everyone agrees with this, and some people argue that morality is a completely artificial social construct. But Harris makes the point that even if we do not currently know all the details of what is necessary to maximize human well-being, we can begin the search with a scientific approach. For further reading on the subject of morality from a scientific perspective, Harris' book is an excellent starting point.

Moral relativism based on religious concepts of morality

When we point out that people's morals have changed significantly over time, we are also acknowledging that the behaviors we now consider wrong were once considered acceptable. People raised in those societies acted according to the values with which they were raised. Does that mean that it was *not* wrong to torture people and animals for fun, but it is now? Or that deliberate genocide *was* acceptable? Part of the reason people engaged in those behaviors was that they didn't know any better, because they didn't understand the nature of suffering or that all human beings are the same species and are closely related. The discoveries of science have helped to inform our moral sense and our sense of justice and leads to the conclusion that it is no longer acceptable to engage in those acts of cruelty. For example, throughout history, people have justified slavery by citing the Bible and by holding a belief that some groups of people are less human than other groups. We now know that is not true, and most of us would agree that it is not right for one human being to own another.

Here is another example. Historically in Western society, there was recognition of a certain degree of sovereignty in an individual household; some matters were considered not to be the concern of outsiders or of the legal system. The man was usually considered the head of the household and was granted certain rights within that household, which included dominion over his family. If he chose to beat his wife,[43] or his children (even severely) it was considered his right. In ancient Rome, parents could legally kill their children.[44]

Today we not only recognize that this is not morally right, but it is against the law; a person using violence against their spouse or child is committing a crime. In societies where this is recognized, no one can successfully use the defense that what happens within the family is nobody else's business. We recognized the right of society, acting through the law, to use force to prevent this behavior.

There are some today who would argue that people in one culture do not have the right to impose their values on another group of people. This kind of moral relativism ignores the progress we have made in our understanding of what it means to be a human, or to be any sentient being, and can be used to justify cruelty and oppression.

Using a naturalist, humanistic morality includes the understanding that certain acts and ways of treating human beings are no longer acceptable, regardless of the culture in which one was raised. If some groups of people do not understand this, it is not necessarily the fact that they are evil; they may simply be uninformed. The effort to educate people about the reality of suffering, or the current standards of human rights, does not automatically constitute an inappropriate attempt to impose your culture on them.

In some cultures today, it is still socially acceptable and legal to commit acts against others that we would consider violations of human rights, such as the severe oppression of people based on their gender, age, sexual orientation, race, ethnicity or religious beliefs. In many cases, these acts are justified by religious belief, and some people argue that what people do within their own system of religious beliefs is no one else's business, or even deserves respect. In contrast, in a moral system based on a naturalistic worldview and scientific principles, it could be justified to insist that everyone obey certain universal standards of behavior towards others, even if it is compelled by law . This includes not allowing slavery, which still goes on in parts of the world. The United States Civil War was fought, at least partly, to impose an end to slavery. Would this be justified on a global scale?

I would argue that while we desire to respect everyone's right to religious freedom, religious justifications do not give a free pass for oppression, murder and genocide. There is no obligation to allow ignorance to justify behavior that violates human rights, and that most people view as abhorrent and no longer permissible.

The Environment

Another important aspect of ethics is how we treat the environment and care for the planet. While the responsibility to care for the environment is part of the spiritual values of many religious groups, some people whose worldview is based on religion believe that we do not need to care for the environment or other species because God created the world for humans to use for their own purposes and God will decide the outcome. Here are examples from a young-Earth creationist that you, as an educated person, may find to be particularly irresponsible.

> The resources given by God at the beginning are enough to sustain us until Christ returns, even if that is another 6,000 years and 50 billion people. Hence, our existence and use of the resources on earth will not change our globe appreciably.

Unless you are willing to deny God's explicit word, you must accept that mankind, no matter what it does, is not going to cause GW/CC [*Global Warming/Climate Change*]. It is not possible.

It is time for Christians to accept God's truth and teach it to their children: God has given us this planet and everything in it to use for our benefit and the exercise of such is not going to harm this world.

—Steven F. Deaton[45]

On the other hand, secular people often see humans as having a moral responsibility to care for the environment. While this view is certainly shared by some religious philosophies, people with a scientific worldview appreciate the value of the evidence and the possible consequences of unrestrained damage to the planet. Human-caused damage to the environment, including global warming, has the potential to not only hurt humans but to cause a catastrophic mass extinction of much of the life on Earth. This is one example of a "spiritual" perspective for non-theists, as it derives not only from the value we place on evidence, but from our sense that we are not the center of the universe, that it was not created for our benefit, and that the scientific evidence shows that we are capable of seriously damaging the delicate ecological balance of the planet. It is not necessary to follow a religious directive in order to believe we have a moral and ethical obligation to care for the environment.

Compare the above statements by Steven Deaton with this from the principles of World Pantheism, a spiritual worldview based on scientific naturalism.

We are an integral part of Nature, which we should cherish, revere and preserve in all its magnificent beauty and diversity. We should strive to live in harmony with Nature locally and globally. We acknowledge the inherent value of all life, human and non-human, and strive to treat all living beings with compassion and respect.[46]

This difference is not one of morality and aesthetics alone—if we do not plan for reducing our damage to the planet, we may have nowhere hospitable to live.

Part IV—Death and the afterlife

...such a deity sprang from infantile yearnings for a powerful, protective father, for justice and fairness and for life to go on forever. God is simply a projection of these desires, feared and worshipped by human beings out of an abiding sense of helplessness.

—Sigmund Freud

One of the unique attributes of humans that distinguishes us from all other life on Earth is the awareness of our own mortality. The knowledge that everyone dies is in one sense a "curse" that we all must live with. Children usually become aware of the inevitability of death at about 5 years old, and it can be very difficult for them to accept. Adults, eager to ease the child's distress, may find it simplest to tell the child that you will not actually die, but you will go to heaven. In fact, many adults are also unable to face the reality of their own mortality and seek similar comfort in tales of an afterlife. You may know someone who has said, "If I didn't believe there was a heaven after we die, I couldn't go on from day to day."

It is part of the process of life on Earth that everything dies, and everything eats and is eaten. All living things that don't use photosynthesis (called heterotrophs) must eat, and what they eat is either living things or the products of living things. Many plants even have mechanisms to protect themselves from being eaten. As a result, all animals in the wild are constantly on guard against being killed and eaten. This is such a high priority that nothing demands more immediate attention than a potential threat to one's existence. For example, what happens if you try approaching a wild squirrel? Even with food in your outstretched hand, you can't get close. A squirrel cannot choose to ignore the immediate potential threat to its life in order to take the food. Similarly, humans, who are also animals and the product of hundreds of millions of years of natural selection, cannot ignore a threat to our lives. The difficulty comes from the fact that once you become aware of the inevitability of your death this essentially constitutes an ongoing "threat" to your life. The fact that this is rather abstract, presumably far off, and not as immediate as a moose charging you, does not reduce the ultimate threat, which is very difficult to ignore. We don't know exactly when religion originated in humans, but we usually consider the earliest evidence of belief in an afterlife, such as grave goods, to be evidence for the origins of religion. It is quite likely that one reason religion and a belief in an afterlife were invented was to help us cope with the knowledge of our own mortality. Studies show that the more people fear death the more likely they are to be religious.[47]

What does science know about death and the afterlife? When people talk about "life after death" they are more accurately referring to some persistence of one's consciousness after death. This is based on the (pre-scientific) idea that the mind and the body are separate entities, and that when the body dies, the mind, (or soul) might continue.

Mind-body duality

In popular culture, we often see expressions of the premise that the mind and the body are distinct entities. Whether it's the idea of a soul that survives the death of the body or "Freaky Friday" stories about individuals swapping minds, we frequently encounter the assumption that mind and body are two different things. The 17th century philosopher and mathematician Rene Descartes is often associated with this philosophy of mind-body dualism, and it is still a very active subject of philosophy.

In 1848, while blasting rock for the railroad, an accident drove an iron bar through the head of Phineas Gage, largely destroying the left frontal lobe of his brain. He survived and lived twelve more years. Reports of changes to his personality, although they vary as to the extent, are credited with beginning the scientific understanding of the role of the brain, rather than of a spirit or a soul, in personality and consciousness. Today, neuroscience does not recognize a duality of mind and body but considers the mind and consciousness to be the result of cellular activity in the brain.

The complete dependence of mental functions on brain processes can be seen in many examples. First, there is clear correspondence between increasing complexity of brain structure and corresponding complexity of cognition across the animal kingdom and across individual human development. Many aspects of human mental functioning have been tied to negative or positive electrical activity generated by specific parts of the brain at specific times. For example, the first visual or auditory information coming into the nervous system reaches the cortex in around 40-100 thousandths of a second, and shortly after that, the individual has a conscious experience of the stimulus. When someone has a seizure involving the whole brain, they lose consciousness, and the loss and regaining of consciousness can be seen in the electrical tracing of brain activity. Conversely, when the brain is stimulated in a specific site, the individual often has a predictable experience (for example, you can make their hand twitch, or make them see checkerboards, or experience a certain emotion). When a part of the brain is irretrievably lost through a stroke, a degenerative disease, a trauma, etc., the mental consequences are fairly predictable. For example, when you lose your left hemisphere, you are likely to have severe deficits in language. It gets even more specific than that: when you lose the front part of your left hemisphere, you are likely to have difficulty speaking but have relatively preserved comprehension; when you lose part of your left hemisphere about a third of the way back, you will likely have particular difficulty in comprehending language. When you lose the fibers that connect these two regions, you will likely have particular difficulty in repeating language that you hear. When you lose a part of your temporal lobe, you will no longer visually recognize loved ones, although you may recognize them when they speak.

When you lose cortical function but still have some functioning of your brainstem (the lowest part of the brain), you may continue to breath and live, but might well be in a permanent coma with no evidence of conscious experience. When the brain totally ceases to function, consciousness and life end.

If you adopt a scientific, naturalistic worldview it means you require evidence before you accept any claims involving the natural world. There is no evidence whatsoever for the persistence of the mind after physical death. Nobody has ever been proven to contact anyone from "beyond the grave" and there is no evidence for the existence of ghosts. People who claim to be able to detect ghosts or to speak to the dead (and have them speak back!) are either entertainers, con artists or delusional. No such claim has ever stood up to careful examination, and no information has ever been revealed from "ghosts" that couldn't have been determined through other means. This is not just a matter of opinion nor is it a case of "there are two sides to every story." For ghosts and an afterlife to exist, much of what science has learned about life, physiology and physics would have to be spectacularly wrong. Professional illusionists, from Harry Houdini to James Randi to Penn and Teller, have demonstrated the ease with which people can be deceived about contact with the afterlife. There are no ghosts, period.

We have all heard stories of people who report having been "dead" and then returning with stories of their experience. Reports of "near death" or "out of the body" experiences are now known to be the result of the way the brain functions under anesthesia or during oxygen deprivation. Nobody has died, "gone to heaven," and returned to life to report about it, despite their subjective belief that this is what happened to them.[48] In fact, researchers have simulated such experiences using electrodes to stimulate a specific part of the right cortex of the brain.[49]

In 2014, Kevin Malarkey and his son Alex published a book entitled *The Boy Who Came Back from Heaven: A Remarkable Account of Miracles, Angels, and Life Beyond This World* in which they claimed that Alex died in a car accident, experienced heaven, and came back to life. In January 2015, Alex admitted that he had fabricated the story and the publisher retracted the book.[50]

The school of philosophy of the the Greek philosopher Epicurus (born 341 BC) and his follower Lucretius (born 94 BC, and the author of the remarkable *On the Nature of Things*), taught that "death is nothing to us" and that people should not fear punishment by the gods after death, because the mind is just part of the body, it will not exist after death, and there will be no suffering. Contrary to what modern people often feel, they taught that the total dissolution of the person should be a comfort.

Is there a "life force" or "life energy"?

There is also no evidence for anything like a "life force." Physics has identified four forces of nature: electromagnetism, gravity, the weak nuclear force and the strong nuclear force.[51] If any other force exists, such as a "universal life force," qi (or chi), vital energy, prana, or "The Force" (sorry, Star Wars fans), there is no evidence for it. And various forms of "energy healing" such as Reiki and therapeutic touch are based on "vitalism," a pre-scientific concept that is essentially a belief in magic. Repeated studies have demonstrated conclusively that any beneficial outcomes these therapies appear to produce are due to the placebo effect.

A placebo is something that a patient believes has medical effectiveness but does not. The placebo effect occurs when the patient experiences a response to a placebo. Some of these effects can be psychological, but there is evidence that some physiological responses may be produced by placebos. For example, placebo pain-killers may elicit the release of endorphins, which are natural pain-killers produced by the brain. Placebos are most effective for subjective experiences, such as pain and mood.

If someone claims to have psychic powers, such as the ability to read minds, predict the future or converse with the dead, they are proposing something that requires the existence of forces that have never been detected. Experiences in which someone was thinking of a person they hadn't seen for a while and then received a call from that person are coincidences, not "ESP" (Extrasensory Perception—psychic abilities such as telepathy and clairvoyance). We remember those events but not the hundreds of times we think of someone and nothing unusual happens. In other words, we count the hits but ignore the misses.

What does happen when you die?

A living organism is a functioning system, made of cells, which uses instructions carried in DNA to harness energy to organize molecules and to reproduce. Once that system has ceased to function (death), all its functions also cease. The matter that comprises that system can no longer be kept in the highly organized state that constitutes a living organism. But the atoms and molecules do not cease to exist. Everything is recycled through incorporation into other living things, either by being eaten by multicellular creatures or in the process of decay. Although some dead bodies are preserved through embalming, most of those will also eventually decay. Decay simply means that microorganisms such as bacteria and fungi consume the molecules and minerals that made up the organism. The energy contained in the chemical bonds of those molecules is used to reorganize the atoms into the structure of the consuming organism. Ultimately, the carbon in organic molecules ends up as carbon dioxide, and the other minerals are also recycled. The carbon dioxide enters the atmosphere and is incorporated into plants using solar energy, whereupon the cycle continues. If a body is cremated, it simply becomes carbon dioxide and minerals that much sooner.

What this means is that you, and all living things, are a temporary arrangement of atoms. These atoms came from other living things and will continue to become part of other living things.

This has been going on for as long as life has existed on Earth, at least 3.8 billion years.

What endures?

What part of your life can survive your death if your "soul" does not continue after your body dies? There are two aspects to this question. First, what part of your "spirit" survives? Second, what physical component of your body survives?

Here we are using the word spirit to mean something other than a soul or ghost or consciousness, which is the metaphysical meaning. There is a different kind of spirit, the metaphorical meaning. The word spirit is sometimes used to mean the essence of something. We can speak of the feeling one gets when experiencing the unique qualities of a place, such as the spirit of New England in the fall or the spirit of Paris. It can also be said that there is a spirit of a culture or of a group of people, such as the spirit of your school or club. We also talk about the spirit of the law, meaning its purpose and intent rather than the exact wording of the statutes. There is an essential quality of a person that is comprised of their personality, their works and the effect they have had on people who have known them, either directly or indirectly. When the comedian and actor Robin Williams died in 2014, many people (even millions who had never met him) felt his spirit had touched them, not through a ghost or magical force that lives on, but by his works, his public personality and his legacy. So, your spirit lives on in your works and in the memories of people who knew you.

What about physically? What part of your physical being survives? As we have already described, all the atoms and molecules of your body will continue to be part of other living things. The physical components of your body are only on temporary loan. While there is no reincarnation of your "soul," you will be "reborn" in many plants and animals. And the atoms and molecules that make up your body have had "past lives" in the sense that they have all been part of other living things. Not only is this true for the well-known fact that "you are what you eat," but goes back through the eons of life on Earth, and before. Not only are there parts of you that were inside stars, but there are also parts of you that were in dinosaurs, trees, and theoretically even the body of George Washington.

There is another sense in which a physical part of who you are continues after you, and that is in the DNA of your children and their children, and in other relatives. Your DNA is the unique instruction set that describes you as an organism. If you have children, you contribute half your DNA to them, and the other parent contributes the other half. Although this results in a new, unique genetic combination in the total DNA of the child, it contains half of your genome. Other relatives also share part of your genome; for example, your siblings share half your DNA, your nieces and nephews share about one-fourth, and first cousins contain about an eighth of your genome. If you don't have children, but contribute to the care and survival of nieces, nephews, siblings or cousins, you are still helping your genes survive.

You are unique

Your genome is one of the most important things that make you the unique individual that you are. This is the DNA instruction set that resides in each of the many trillions of cells of your body. There are 3 billion "letters" or base pairs in your DNA, and this exact combination is unique in the world and throughout history. No person has ever lived with your exact DNA, except if you have an identical twin, and it cannot continue in its present form no matter how successful it is. Not just do we have to die but that DNA combination cannot continue even in a new "vehicle," other than through cloning, which has never yet been done with humans. So in that sense, every one of us is a unique individual. Even identical twins, who share the same chromosomal DNA set, have some differences such as their fingerprints, as well as slight changes due to environment and another layer of genetic complexity known as *epigenetics*.

This scientific understanding of your place in the order of life on Earth has implications that many find spiritual.

1- You are unique and special, right now and in the history of life on Earth.
2- Given the conditions necessary for life to exist, for humans to have evolved, and for you to have been born you are in essence the winner of a cosmic lottery whose odds of winning are much less than any Powerball

jackpot.

3- In the vastness of cosmic time, this is the one chance you will get for life. Because there is no afterlife or reincarnation of your spirit, you must make the most of what you have in this life. This will be your only chance to enjoy existence, to do some good, and to leave a legacy.

Part V—Secular versions of traditional religion functions

Holidays and rituals

A common function of traditional religions has been to provide ceremonies and rituals to mark significant times of the year and important milestones of life, as well as a sense of community with those around you. There is some evidence that people who regularly attend religious services may recover more quickly from illness or injury and may even live longer. But psychologists and physicians who study this phenomenon suggest that having a network of social support, a sense of optimism and purpose, and resulting reductions in stress from churchgoing may be responsible for this effect. So consider whether you have a network of social support of family and friends, whether it is based on religion, culture, beliefs, activities, or something else.

Holidays

In the same way that many ancient religious rites were adapted for Christianity, secular people can repurpose those same rituals for secular celebrations, thereby celebrating the harvest season, the solstice or the arrival of springtime, through special meals and a gathering with family and friends.

Many religious holidays are derived from the need to recognize recurring events in the solar year. Marking the seasons helps acknowledge important tasks such as when to plant crops and when to prepare for winter. In pre-scientific belief systems, it serves to placate the gods or to ask them for help or to prevent disasters. Most modern religious holidays are more recent versions of annual observances that existed long before the specific religion to which they are now attributed, and many of the annual observances are common to many cultures and religions today. For example, the Roman pagan celebrations around the winter solstice, Brumalia and Saturnalia, were subsequently adapted into the Christian Christmas celebration. Some pagan celebrations of spring are associated with the Germanic goddess Eostre, after whom Easter is named.

Cultures around the world mark the winter solstice.[52] In the northern hemisphere, this is the time when the noon sun is at its lowest point above the horizon and is the shortest daylight period of the year. As a result, most of these observances are festivals of light[53] and have a theme of defying darkness and the winter. Some additional aspects of the Christmas celebration, such as the evergreen tree, are likely also derived from other pagan religious observances of the solstice. The Jewish winter solstice festival of lights, Hanukah, is based on a legend that after a revolt against Hellenistic occupation of Judea in the second century B.C., the oil lights used in the rededication of the temple, instead of lasting only one day as expected, burned for eight days.

Holiday observances around the time of the March equinox, when day and night are equal, mark the end of winter and the time to plant crops.[54] The themes of these celebrations, such as Christian Easter and Jewish Passover, usually center on fertility, resurrection and rebirth as winter ends and the growing season starts. The symbols of spring and fertility that are used, such as eggs, lambs, rabbits and flowers, are also common to many pagan religions.

Must non-theists then reject these observances? Are you being hypocritical if you are not an observant Christian but you enjoy Christmas? Consider this story of an experience the author had when traveling in the Amazon. Our group was invited to visit a village of indigenous people and a traditional welcoming ceremony was performed in our honor. During the ceremony, the Chief put an assortment of leaves and twigs on a plank and placed a burning ember in the middle. He walked around the circle and held the smoldering herbs in front of each visitor, wafting the smoke toward us and instructing us to inhale the vapors. He then spoke an incantation intended to bless our journey and bring us good fortune. This was an ancient religious ritual, based on a belief in spirits of the rain forest. We were honored to participate, and felt a spiritual connection to the people of this tribe and our presence in the rain forest. It did not require us to actually believe in the reality of forest spirits, nor were we offended because it contradicted our beliefs.

The same applies to any religious tradition. You do not need to be a believer in the Christian version of God or the supernatural aspects of Christmas in order to enjoy the celebration of the winter solstice that is Christmas. In fact, many people who are atheists have "Christmas" trees in their homes simply because they enjoy having a festive bit of greenery and sparkle in the winter, and enjoy participating in a holiday that most of their community is observing. Fifty percent of people who consider themselves to be Jewish describe themselves as secular yet 70% observe the spring equinox holiday of Passover by attending the traditional celebratory meal, the Seder.[55] The desire to celebrate the coming of spring, gather with friends and family, and honor an ancient tradition, whether through the observance of Easter, Passover, Naw Ruz (Baha'i), or other practices, are all positive and enjoyable motivations that do not require the belief in supernatural events.

Belonging to a congregation

In Sweden, 57% of the population belongs to the Lutheran Church of Sweden; yet only 18% of the population says they believe that there is a God.[56] So even church membership does not necessarily mean that you are committing to a belief in God. There are many reasons for joining an organized religious community that are compatible with a secular worldview.

Rituals for life passages

People have always had ceremonies and rituals, also called rites of passage, to mark the important transitions of life: birth and baby naming, puberty rites, marriage ceremonies, funeral observances. There are also many secular rites of passage, such as graduation ceremonies, inaugurations and retirement parties. There is certainly value in marking important transitions and anniversaries in our lives, and involving other people to be with us at these times. For this purpose, ceremonies derived from religious practices are still meaningful and many secular people still find spiritual meaning and significance in participating in them. The World Pantheism movement provides many suggestions of non-theistic yet spiritual forms of celebration.[57] As with holidays, you can participate in a religious ceremony even if you don't believe in the supernatural religious aspect, such as a baby naming, or the religious versions of these ceremonies can be adapted for secular use by removing references to God and the supernatural and substituting your own secular beliefs.

Some of the communities described below such as American Humanist Association, Ethical Culture and Humanists UK have "celebrants" or "officiants" who are trained to officiate at secular versions of ceremonies such as weddings, funerals, baby namings, etc.

Community

One common interpretation of the origin of the word religion is that it means to rebind or reconnect, from the Latin word *ligare*, to bind or connect. Regardless of the exact etymology of the word, there is no question that one function of religion is to bring people together in communities. Many people are satisfied to remain unaffiliated and to seek their own path to a non-theistic spirituality. Others maintain ties with their own religious communities, despite not believing their tenets, or not believing them literally. Others prefer to affiliate with a community of like-minded people who identify themselves as secular humanists; some of these groups are "congregational" and meet on a regular basis, while others do not have such regular, "congregational" meetings but function as active organizations that promote and organize humanist activities.

Many people belong to a religious congregation because they derive comfort from belonging to a community of people with shared beliefs and/or traditions. Many religious groups that are congregationalist (that is, groups that have regular assemblies) are accepting of a range of beliefs among their congregants. Some secular people who want to find a spiritual community choose to belong to a Unitarian Universalist congregation. While Unitarianism is considered a religion, it is very inclusive, and many members of Unitarian communities are atheist or agnostic. The denominations of Judaism known in the U.S. as Reform Judaism, Reconstructionist Judaism and Secular Humanist Judaism[58] count, among their congregants, many people whose interest is in belonging to a group of people who share a common cultural experience and traditions, but who do not subscribe specifically to the supernatural beliefs of the more orthodox denominations.

Other communities are explicitly humanist or secular but have regular assemblies of their members; these include Ethical Humanism (also called Ethical Culture), Sunday Assembly, and Oasis. Ethical Culture Society members are dedicated to social justice causes including promoting the rights of women, minorities, the poor and the working class. Societies are located in 14 American states but are concentrated in the NY metropolitan area. While they function as ethical communities rather than as congregations per se, many do have meetings on Sundays. For Ethical Humanists, the ultimate religious questions are not about the existence of gods or an afterlife, but rather, "How can we create meaningfulness in this life?" and "How should we treat each other?" expressed in the phrase "Deed before Creed."[59]

Sunday Assembly provides a congregation with meetings for non-religious people who desire the formal community structure that this provides. It was founded in 2013 in London, where meetings are held twice a month. Meetings have also been held in other UK cities, in the US (New York, Pittsburgh, Los Angeles), Germany, the Netherlands, Australia, Canada, New Zealand, and Hungary.

Oasis network[60] is another non-faith-based community that provides weekly Sunday meetings, with talks, music, and chance for discussion, as well as interest groups and social justice activities at other times. Current locations for Oasis groups are in Texas, Utah, Kansas City, and Toronto; their website describes procedures for starting your own Oasis group with as few as five people.

Other organizations follow less of the traditional model of weekly or monthly meetings, but function as groups dedicated to humanist causes. There are several philosophical approaches that use the term "humanism" but have in common beliefs that are expressed in the definition of Humanism from the American Humanist Association:

> **Humanism** is a progressive philosophy of life that, without theism or other supernatural beliefs, affirms our ability and responsibility to lead ethical lives of personal fulfillment that aspire to the greater good.
>
> – *American Humanist Association*

One example of such a group is found in Secular Humanism.[61] The term "secular humanism" was adapted by Paul Kurtz in the context of his organization The Center for Inquiry. This is from the website of the Council for Secular Humanism:[62]

Secular humanism is a comprehensive, nonreligious life stance incorporating:

- A naturalistic philosophy
- A cosmic outlook rooted in science
- A consequentialist ethical system

As the above bullets indicate, Secular Humanism incorporates the philosophy of the scientific worldview, an approach to meaning and perspective consistent with science, and a sense of morality based on results rather than orders from gods. The website has much valuable information about the community and provides links to groups.

The American Humanist Association (AHA) is an educational advocacy organization serving the spectrum of humanists from atheist to secular to religious and everything in between. It fosters community in building local chapters and affiliates around the country. Indeed, the AHA is involved in working hard to advance the humanist point of view—the idea that you can be good without a belief in a god. Together with their connected organizations, and with a good online presence, they advocate and argue for humanist values: defending the separation between church and state, advancing humanist thought in education, providing aid to those most in need, encouraging the application of humanism to daily life, and affirming humanism's commitment to working toward social justice.

There are many other North American atheist and humanist organizations. A sampling is: American Atheists,[63] founded by Madalyn Murray O'Hair; it focuses on absolute separation of church and state, and the legal rights of atheists.

The Freedom from Religion Foundation[64] takes legal action in separation of church and state cases, provides speakers, puts out educational material, and sponsors an annual freethinkers' convention. It has chapters in 20 US states.

The Secular Student Alliance[65] is the only national organization dedicated to atheist and humanist students on college campuses and high schools. They have chapters in every US state, and work to make students proud of non-theist communities, promote secular values, publish a newsletter, and support activities of local chapters.

International Organizations

Most of the organizations described above are concentrated in the US and Canada (except for Sunday Assembly, which was founded in London). Other important organizations and sources of information for Humanism outside the US include the British Humanist Association and Humanists International.

The British Humanist Association (also known as Humanists UK[66]) was founded in 1896, currently has over 85,000 members and supports all aspects of humanism in the U.K. It stresses helping oneself and others, to make the most of "the one life we have," through promoting progressive education, secular government, human rights and equality, and ethical issues (e.g., abortion rights and assisted dying). It also trains celebrants who can officiate at non-religious ceremonies such as marriages and funerals.

Humanists International (also known as the International

Humanist and Ethical Union) is the global representative body of the humanist movement, uniting a diversity of non-religious organizations and individuals. Members include more than 160 humanist, rationalist, secular, ethical culture, atheist and freethought organizations in more than 70 countries. "We campaign on humanist issues. We defend humanists at risk of persecution and violence. We lobby for humanist values at international institutions, including the United Nations. And we work to build the humanist movement around the world."[67] Humanist International publishes a yearly "freedom of thought" report, updating readers on discrimination against non-theists such as contained in "blasphemy laws," has a youth organization, promotes democratic international law, and has a world congress yearly convention.

Scientific pantheism

Pantheism is a philosophy associated with the 17th-century philosopher Baruch Spinoza. It is based on a naturalistic worldview that concludes that "god" is the totality of the natural world ("nature"), in its physical manifestations and in its laws and behavior. The World Pantheism Movement[68] has a website that is a good starting point to investigate this philosophy.

Naturalism

The strict belief that the universe consists of only matter and energy and their interactions, and that there are no "spirits" or supernatural entities is called metaphysical naturalism. This philosophy is similar to pantheism. Organizations that provide support and community include the Center for Naturalism.[69]

Here is a summary from their blog:[70]

Worldview Naturalism in a Nutshell

If you don't believe in anything supernatural—gods, ghosts, immaterial souls and spirits—then you subscribe to naturalism, the idea that nature is all there is. The reason you're a naturalist is likely that, wanting not to be deceived, you put stock in empirical, evidence-based ways of justifying beliefs about what's real, as for instance exemplified by science. You probably (and rightly) hold that such beliefs are usually more reliable and more objective than those based in uncorroborated intuition, revelation, religious authority or sacred texts. Kept honest by philosophy and critical thinking, science reveals a single manifold of existence, what we call nature, containing an untold myriad of interconnected phenomena, from quarks to quasars. Nature is simply what we have good reason to believe exists.

Flying Spaghetti Monster

On a lighter note, the Church of the Flying Spaghetti Monster began as a parody of religion that makes the point that there is no more evidence to believe in the claims of traditional religions, including the belief that God created the world in six days (creationism) than there is to believe in a supreme being made of spaghetti and meatballs. If you are looking for a more humorous approach to religion, they have a website.[71]#

Dealing with adversity

We too need to get over the questions that focus on the past and on the pain—"why did this happen to me?"—and ask instead the question which opens doors to the future: "Now that this has happened, what shall I do about it?"

—Rabbi Harold Kushner

In his book, *When Bad Things Happen to Good People*, Harold Kushner takes the position that God does not interfere with the laws of nature, and sometimes bad things happen for random reasons. His premise is that once you accept the idea that a tragedy did not happen because you deserved it, you can get on with your life and use the experience to find meaning in your future. This reasoning is also compatible with a secular worldview. There is no need to understand why God lets bad things happen to you if the answer is: God had nothing to do with it. Adversity is not a punishment from God if you don't believe there is a God. You do not need to ask yourself what you did to deserve this misfortune. Neither is good fortune a reward from God. After a natural disaster, such as a tornado, you will often see an interview with someone whose house was spared when all around were flattened. The person then thanks God for sparing his house. But what did God have against his neighbors? If both football teams pray to God to help them win, does anyone really believe that a God would care which team wins and that he would actually interfere with the outcome?

The subconscious belief that people somehow get what they "deserve" is generally referred to as the *Just World Hypothesis*. It is a form of cognitive bias that may help people cope with the fact that most good and bad fortune is random and not a reward or punishment from God, Karma or other supernatural forces. When we hear that someone died of cancer or in a car accident, we may ask "Were they a smoker?" or "Were they wearing their seatbelt?" This tendency to "blame the victim" may help people believe they have a modicum of control over such events.

Related to this is the "problem of evil," which has faced theologians and philosophers since ancient times.[72] How could a god who is all-powerful, all-knowing and also benevolent allow evil to exist? If he was powerful enough, he would be able to do something about it; knowledgeable enough, he would know what to do about it; benevolent enough, he would want to do something about it. And yet suffering and evil still plentifully exist. The atheist argument is that the existence of evil is incompatible with the existence of a god with all those attributes. There are many attempts to explain this by religious apologists, including invoking a "devil," which is little more than an adaptation of a polytheistic belief in good gods and bad gods (which itself carries many problems, not least the idea that if God was all-powerful, he could do away with the devil in the blink of an eye, yet the devil supposedly remains to carry out his evil.)

The point is that misfortune is not part of God's plan, it is not punishment or reward, and it is not the work of the devil. It's often the result of simple bad luck. Of course, atheists also acknowledge that our actions have consequences and sometimes misfortunes are our own fault. Since this is our only life and our one chance to get it right, we must think carefully about the consequences of our actions for others and for ourselves. For a non-theistic perspective on dealing with loss, the actor, comedian and atheist Ricky Gervais has created a critically acclaimed series for Netflix called *After Life*. It's worth watching.

Awe, Humility and Mystery

The first chapter of this work begins with a quote from Carl Sagan:

> Science is not only compatible with spirituality; it is a profound source of spirituality. When we recognize our place in an immensity of light-years and in the passage of ages, when we grasp the intricacy, beauty and subtlety of life, then that soaring feeling, that sense of elation and humility combined, is surely spiritual.

People often describe a spiritual experience as involving a sense of the loss of self, the feeling that you are part of a much greater whole. Perhaps you can experience this by looking up at a star-filled sky (or visiting a planetarium), standing on top of a high peak and seeing a distant view, walking in the woods, listening to music or enjoying art. If you are a metaphysical naturalist, and therefore you believe that the natural world is all there is, then being in a place where you can experience a perspective on how vast nature is and how small you (and your problems) are can have a very calming and focusing effect, which many would describe as spiritual.

Many atheists also find spiritual meaning in the sense that they are extremely lucky to be alive. The probability of your existence is so small that it is essentially near zero. What had to happen in order for you to exist? Let's skip past questions of the events that led to the existence of this universe with the current physical laws and simply take that as given. A habitable planet is required, which means conditions such as the mass and gravity must be within a suitable range, orbiting a sun-like star at a distance where the necessary amount of energy falls on the planet, and a temperature range that allows liquid water to exist. There are likely to be many such planets in our galaxy.[73] The Earth formed about 4.5 billion years ago, and life appeared about 3.5-3.8 billion years ago. Since life appeared on Earth fairly soon after the formation of the planet, astronomers and biologists assume that bacteria-like life is not rare in the galaxy. While estimates of the number of planets supporting life are largely conjecture, one estimate (the Drake equation) suggests there might be 6 billion planets with the capacity to support life in the known universe.[74]

However, biologists and astronomers part ways in their estimates of the existence of *intelligent* life.

Many of the events in the history of life on Earth were unique or of low probability. For example, it took about 3 billion years after the appearance of life for multicellular organisms to appear, which suggests that just the transition to multi-cellularity may itself be a rare event. There have been five known mass extinctions in which most of the life on Earth disappeared, significantly changing the balance of life and the mix of species. The last such event, the asteroid that impacted the Earth at the end of the Cretaceous period about 65 million years ago and likely led to the extinction of the dinosaurs was a random and unpredictable event. If not for that, mammals might never have flourished. Yet since then, no similarly catastrophic event has interrupted the path that led to the evolution of humans (possibly due to the fact that the massive gravity of Jupiter may protect the earth from more numerous such events). There are many similarly lucky incidents, such as the change in climate in Africa that caused the formation of savannah where there had been forest, so that some apes took to walking upright, which allowed them to see farther and cover greater distances in the search for food. Of our many human-like ancestors, no other species has survived to the present day except *Homo sapiens sapiens.*

Even taking the existence of human beings as a given (and that's a significant assumption), for you to exist, none of your ancestors going back to the first bacterial life has died before reproducing. Even taking the meeting of your parents as a given, your specific life required just one of tens of millions of sperm to have succeeded in fertilizing one particular egg, leading to a successful pregnancy and birth. It is apparent from observing siblings that even the same parents never give rise to the exact same individuals. In Part IV, we discussed the genetic basis for the fact that each person is absolutely unique, has never existed before and will almost certainly never exist again.

Surely, this understanding (scientific and naturalistic) should be a source of awe and humility. Understanding what a low probability event your life is can inspire you to try to make the most of it. There are many works that celebrate the wonder that comes from an appreciation of the vastness of the universe, the unimaginable span of time that preceded your arrival, and how staggeringly unlikely is your own existence. Some recommended videos and books relevant to this are listed before the references.

Something Larger

Theists often ask non-theists whether they don't need to feel that they are part of "something larger" than themselves. The implication is that a God and "His plan" is something larger, and that if you believe that the natural world is all there is then you don't have a larger perspective than yourself. The fact is that people with a scientific worldview have a great many resources upon which to draw in gaining perspective on the larger reality of the universe and a more accurate view of just how big and how old it is!

For thousands of years, followers of the Abrahamic religions have believed people to be created in God's image and that the universe (and everything in it) was created by God for the benefit of human beings. This not only included the belief that the sun revolved around the earth but that we were the center of the entire universe, both literally and metaphorically. In contrast, the scientific explanation sees humans as existing on a tiny point in a vast universe and views our existence as not necessarily unique. Not only are we not the center of the solar system, but we aren't even near the center of our galaxy, and the current estimate is that there are about 2 trillion galaxies. The known universe is about 46 billion light-years in diameter.[75] How's that for something larger? And this might not be the only universe![76] In fact, secularists feel that the idea that we are all there is and the universe exists just for us is a much smaller and more limited view, not a larger one.

Great Mysteries

While science has contributed so much to our knowledge of the natural world, there are still many great mysteries of which we have only the most preliminary understanding. Science does not regard these as impenetrable, only yet to be explored.

1- How did the universe begin? What came before? Are there other universes?

2- How did life originate on Earth? Evolution only explains how life *changed* once it appeared. Explanations of how it began are largely speculative (this is called abiogenesis).

3- How does human intelligence work? How does a collection of neurons, whose function at the cellular level is the same in all creatures, lead to human consciousness and abstract reasoning? Can we build a machine with human-like intelligence?

4- Is there other life in the universe? Is there other *intelligent* life in the universe? Why haven't we found evidence when it seems likely that other intelligent life exists?

5- Can we stop or reverse aging?

6- Can we create life in the laboratory?

There are more. Go online and check them out or, better still, sit and ponder these big questions yourself and wonder what needs answering.

What is the meaning of life?

> …every one of our body's atoms is traceable to the Big Bang and to the thermonuclear furnace within high-mass stars. We are not simply in the universe; we are part of it. We are born from it. One might even say we have been empowered by the universe to figure itself out—and we have only just begun.
>
> —Neil deGrasse Tyson[77]

In order to approach this question of the meaning of life, we must first define what it means. Here are some interpretations of that

76

question and suggested answers. We'll start with the simplest one.

What does "life" mean on this planet? Life on Earth is a system that captures energy from the sun and uses it to organize matter into self-replicating units using the instructions contained in DNA.

Is there a purpose to life on Earth? This implies a God or other creator who made life on Earth for a reason. In the absence of a creator, the scientific answer would be no, life seems to have occurred as a random event.

Is there a purpose to your own life? Is there a purpose to human existence? Again, there is no evidence for a creator who intended humans to carry out a "mission," and evolution indicates that humans appeared as a result of random events and natural selection. So, in *that* sense the answer is still no, there is no preordained purpose to human existence, no purpose given by something outside of ourselves, outside of the universe.

However, although a purpose is not predetermined, sometimes circumstances result in an opportunity to find meaning. Consider the organization Mothers Against Drunk Driving (MADD.org.). In 1980, Candace Lightner's daughter Cari was killed by a drunk driver who had multiple previous convictions for drunk driving. From this horrible tragedy, Mrs. Lightner founded Mothers Against Drunk Driving, which began a national campaign to educate people about the devastating effects of drunk driving and to strengthen laws against driving drunk. In the years since then, MADD estimates that drunk driving has been cut in half. No doubt thousands of lives have been saved as a result of the

MADD campaign. Mrs. Lightner was not preordained to form MADD, nor was it the purpose for which she or Cari were born or the purpose for Cari's tragic death. Circumstances beyond her control presented her with a newfound purpose in life, and a great deal of good for society has come from it.

The generation that was called upon to fight World War Two would almost certainly not have chosen to make that sacrifice if it could have been avoided. But they answered the need, and it is widely accepted that they saved the world from fascism. Because of their sacrifice, they are often referred to as "The Greatest Generation."

The generation of young people today may find themselves faced with another call that represents an existential crisis. Global climate change caused largely by discharging carbon dioxide into the atmosphere over two hundred years of burning fossil fuels represents a threat not only to humans, but to all life on Earth. To prevent this, or at least reduce the effect, will require drastic changes in our ways of doing things. If this generation can rise to the challenge, they may indeed be the "New Greatest Generation."

Purpose and meaning are arguably things that must come from within ourselves. Even if there was a god to dictate to us our purpose, that would not mean it would necessarily be *our* purpose. We would still have to interpret that purpose and meaning for ourselves. It is rather similar to looking at a painting or listening to a song; we generate our own meaning and appreciation for the art. When it comes to the grand ideas of purpose and meaning for our own lives, it is a far more noble endeavor to generate our own meaning in life than to accept a meaning or purpose imposed upon us from elsewhere. We are the authors of our own lives.

Humans are the result of laws of nature acting on inert matter and energy to result in life. Uniquely (on this planet), we have evolved the intelligence to develop not only self-aware consciousness, but also the tools of science to understand the universe. Since we are made of the matter that was formed in the Big Bang and inside stars, and are governed by the laws of matter and energy that are part of the universe, we are truly the universe figuring itself out, or as Carl Sagan said in the television series and book *Cosmos*, "We are a way for the cosmos to know itself." We don't know of any other intelligent life in the universe; we may be alone.

Therefore, it falls to us to take on the mission to understand the universe. Not as a result of a predetermined plan, and due to circumstances beyond our control, we find ourselves as a species presented with a mission, to understand how the natural world works. If one accepts this as at least part of the purpose of human existence, we also have a responsibility to use our intelligence, and the tools of science to cooperate to ensure the survival and well-being of our species and our environment.

Here are some more suggestions:

1- We can work toward greater human cooperation, a course that appears to be necessary for our survival as a species.
2- We can work to get people to accept the scientific worldview as the best path to solve the problems we face.
3- If you come out publicly as a non-theist, which is not always easy to do, you can help others like yourself realize

79

that they're not alone, and help other people to accept non-theists.

4- You can work to prevent a global environmental catastrophe that may occur as the result of human use of fossil fuels.

In addition to this view of a purpose in human existence, individual people can find their own meaning. Whether it is a project like MADD, or simply living your life in a way that contributes to the well-being of other people and the protection of the earth, you can define your own purpose and meaning.

Finally, a sense of spiritual satisfaction can come from the understanding that you are supporting the long human quest for understanding, by supporting the use of science and reason, and rejecting superstition and belief in magic.

Suggested Reading/Viewing

Religion and Non-religion

Carrier, R. (2005) Sense and Goodness without God. Bloomington, Ind: AuthorHouse.

Dawkins, R. (2008) The God Delusion. New York: Mariner Books

Dawkins, R. (2019) Outgrowing God, The Beginner's Guide. New York: Penguin Random House.

Harris, S. (2014) Waking Up: A Guide to Spirituality without Religion. New York: Simon and Schuster.

Harris, S. (2014) The End of Faith. New York: W.W. Norton and Company.

Hitchens, C. (2009) God is Not Great: How Religion Poisons Everything. New York: Hatchette Book Group.

Pearce, J. (ed.) (2017) Not Seeing God: Atheism in the 21st Century. London: Onus Books

Pearce, J. and Vick, T. (2014) Beyond an Absence of Faith: Stories About the Loss of Faith and the Discovery of Self. London: Onus Books.

Historical

Darwin, C. (1859) On the Origin of Species by Means of Natural Selection

Greenblatt, S. (2012) The Swerve: How the World Became Modern. New York: W.W. Norton and Company

Lucretius (2007 Written about 50 BC) On the Nature of Things. New York: Penguin Classics.

Science and Critical Thinking

Bausell, R.B. (2007) Snake Oil Science: The Truth about Complementary and Alternative Medicine. Oxford: Oxford University Press.

Dawkins, R. (2012) The Magic of Reality: How We Know What's Really True. New York: Simon Schuster.

Novella, Steve (2018) The Skeptics Guide to the Universe: How to Know What's Really Real in a World Increasingly Full of Fake. New York: Hatchette Book Group.

Offit, P. MD, (2013) Do You Believe in Magic?: The Sense and Nonsense of Alternative Medicine. New York: Harper Collins.

Offit, P. , MD (2015) Bad Faith: When Religious Belief Undermines Modern Medicine. New York: Basic Books.

Randi, James (1982) Flim-Flam: Psychics, ESP, Unicorns and Other Delusions. New York: Prometheus Books

Schick, Theodore Jr. and Lewis Vaughn (2013) How to Think About Weird Things: Critical Thinking for a New Age 7th Edition. New York: McGraw-Hill Education

Shermer, Michael (2002) Why People Believe Weird Things: Pseudoscience, Superstition, and Other Confusions of Our Time New York: Henry Holt

Singh, S. and Ernst, E., MD (2008) Trick or Treatment: The Undeniable Facts about Alternative Medicine. New York: W.W. Norton and Company.

Sagan, Carl (1996) The Demon-Haunted World: Science as a Candle in the Dark. New York: Ballantine Books

Evolution

Coyne, Jerry A. (2010) Why Evolution Is True. New York: Penguin

Dawkins, R. (2010) The Greatest Show on Earth. New York: Free Press Simon and Schuster.

Marcus, Gary (2008) Kluge: The Haphazard Evolution of the Human Mind. New York: Houghton Mifflin

Harari, Y. (2015) Sapiens: A Brief History of Humankind. New York: Harper Collins.

Video

After Life (2019) Netflix TV series by Ricky Gervais. After losing his wife to cancer a man rediscovers what's really important in life.

The Earth from Space (2013) (Nova, PBS) https://www.pbs.org/wgbh/nova/video/earth-from-space/ Satellite data reveals the interconnectedness of all life on Earth.

Religulous (2008) Documentary film by Bill Maher about religious belief

Atheism United Wiki

https://www.atheismunited.com/wiki/Huge_list_of_atheist_agnostic_skeptic_humanist_websites (accessed Aug. 23, 2019)

References

[1] "How to Determine the Reliability of a Wikipedia Article" https://www.wikihow.com/Determine-the-Reliability-of-a-Wikipedia-Article (accessed Aug. 22, 2019)

[2] Andrei, M. (2014). "Study shows Wikipedia Accuracy is 99.5%" https://www.zmescience.com/science/study-wikipedia-25092014/ (accessed August 13, 2019).

[3] Cox, Daniel & Jones, Robert P. (2017) "America's Changing Religious Identity," https://www.prri.org/research/american-religious-landscape-christian-religiously-unaffiliated/ (accessed August 13, 2019).

[4] Kosmin, Barry. (2014). "Research Report: Secular Students Today," https://commons.trincoll.edu/aris/ (accessed August 13, 2019).

[5] National Academy of Sciences and Institute of Medicine (2008). Science, Evolution, and Creationism. Washington, DC: The National Academies Press.

[6] Moran, Laurence. (2010), "Who's the Grownup in the Sciencs vs. Religion Debate?" http://sandwalk.blogspot.com/2010/03/whos-grownup-in-science-vs-religion.html (accessed August 13, 2019).

[7] Evidence, Internet Encyclopedia of Philosophy, https://www.iep.utm.edu/evidence/#H3 (accessed August 13, 2019).

[8] "What is Metaphysical Naturalism and Methodological Naturalism/" (2011) http://humanists4science.blogspot.com/2011/11/what-is-metaphysical-naturalism.html (accessed August 13, 2019).

[9] Carrier, Richard (2005). Sense and Goodness Without God: A Defense of Metaphysical Naturalism, Bloomington, Indiana: Authorhouse

[10] Schafersman, S. D. (1997), "Naturalism is today an essential part of science." In Conference on Naturalism, Theism, and the Scientific Enterprise. Austin, TX. http://www.stephenjaygould.org/ctrl/schafersman_nat.html (accessed August 13, 2019)..

[11] http://www.people-press.org/2009/07/09/section-4-scientists-politics-and-religion (accessed August 13, 2019).

[12] "Concepts of God" (2012) http://plato.stanford.edu/entries/concepts-god/ (accessed August 13, 2019).

[13] Larson, E. J., & Witham, L. (1998). Leading scientists still reject God. Nature, 394(6691), 313.

[14] Gould, S.J. (1997) Nonoverlapping magisteria, Natural History 106: 16-22

[15] Dawkins, R. (2008). The God Delusion. New York: Mariner Books.

[16] Harris, S. (2014). Waking Up: A Guide to Spirituality without Religion.

New York: Simon and Schuster.

[17] Sagan, C. (1997). The Demon-Haunted World: Science as a Candle in the Dark. New York: Ballantine Books.

[18] Dawkins, R. (2008). The God Delusion. New York: Mariner Books.

[19] Lipka, M. (2016) "Ten facts about atheists." https://www.pewresearch.org/fact-tank/2016/06/01/10-facts-about-atheists/ (accessed August 13, 2019).

[20] "WPM Statement of Principles of Scientific Pantheism." https://www.pantheism.net/manifest/ (accessed August 13, 2019).

[21] "Science for All Americans," Chapter 1, http://www.project2061.org/publications/sfaa/online/sfaatoc.htm/ (accessed August 13, 2019).

[22] www.oxforddictionaries.com/us/definition/american_english/miracle (accessed August 13, 2019).

[23] Greenberg, D., et al (2019). "Increasing Support for Religiously Based Service Refusals" https://www.prri.org/research/increasing-support-for-religiously-based-service-refusals/ (accessed August 13, 2019).

[24] Tortora, B. (2010). "Witchcraft Believers in Sub-Saharan Africa Rate Lives Worse." https://news.gallup.com/poll/142640/witchcraft-believers-sub-saharan-africa-rate-lives-worse.aspx (accessed August 13, 2019).

[25] McCoy, T. (2014). "Thousands of women, accused of sorcery, tortured and executed in Indian witch hunts." https://www.washingtonpost.com/news/morning-mix/wp/2014/07/21/thousands-of-women-accused-of-sorcery-tortured-and-executed-in-indian-witch-hunts/?noredirect=on&utm_term=.6b633ce63b78 (accessed August 13, 2019).

[26] Gott III, J. R., Jurić, M., Schlegel, D., et al (2005). A Map of the Universe. The Astrophysical Journal, 624(2), 463.

[27] Lane, N. (2015) The Vital Question: Energy, Evolution and the Origins of Complex Life. New York: W.W. Norton and Company.

[28] Darwin, C. (1859). On the Origin of Species. London: John Murray.

[29] "Eukaryote" http://en.wikipedia.org/wiki/Eukaryote (accessed August 13, 2019).

[30] Wright, Robert (2001). Non-Zero: The Logic of Human Destiny, New York: Vintage Books.

[31] Watson, J. D., & Crick, F. (1953). A structure for deoxyribose nucleic acid. Nature (3), 171, 737-738.

[32] Masters, Kevin S., Spielmans, Glen I., Goodson, Jason T. (2006) "Are there demonstrable effects of distant intercessory prayer? A meta-analytic review," *Annals of Behavioral Medicine*, 32(1), pp. 21–26, https://doi.org/10.1207/s15324796abm3201_3 (accessed August 13, 2019).

[33] "Efficacy of prayer" https://en.wikipedia.org/wiki/Efficacy_of_prayer (accessed August 13, 2019).

[34] "Vatican backs abortion row bishop" http://news.bbc.co.uk/2/hi/americas/7930380.stm (accessed August 13, 2019).

[35] Harris, S. (2011). The Moral Landscape: How Science Can Determine Human Values. New York: Simon and Schuster. Page 35

[36] "Baruch Spinoza" http://en.wikipedia.org/wiki/Baruch_Spinoza (accessed August 13, 2019).

[37] "Cat-burning" http://en.wikipedia.org/wiki/Cat_burning (accessed August 13, 2019).

[38] Hitchens, C. (2008). God is not great: How religion poisons everything. Toronto: McClelland & Stewart.

[39] Pearce, J. (2019) "A Great Myth about Atheism: Hitler/Stalin/Pol Pot = Atheism = Atrocity – REDUX" (2019) https://www.patheos.com/blogs/tippling/2019/03/24/a-great-myth-about-atheism-hitler-stalin-pol-pot-atheism-atrocity-redux/ (accessed August 13, 2019).

[40] "Catholic Church and Nazi Germany" http://en.wikipedia.org/wiki/Catholic_Church_and_Nazi_Germany (accessed August 13, 2019).

[41] Mikhail, J. (2007). Universal moral grammar: Theory, evidence and the future. Trends in Cognitive Sciences, 11(4), 143-152.

[42] Pearce, J. (2019). "Making Moral Claims: Evolution and Other Animals" https://www.patheos.com/blogs/tippling/2019/05/20/making-moral-claims-the-biosocial-jigsaw/ (accessed August 13, 2019).

[43] "Domestic violence: social and legal concept" http://www.britannica.com/EBchecked/topic/168589/domestic-violence (accessed August 13, 2019).

[44] Harris, W. (1994) Child Exposure in the Roman Empire. Journal of Roman Studies, 84, 1-22.

[45] Deaton, S. "Global Warming: A Biblical View" http://implantedword.com/?s=global+warming (accessed August 13, 2019).

[46] "WPM Statement of Principles of Scientific Pantheism." https://www.pantheism.net/manifest/ (accessed August 13, 2019).

[47] Ellis, L., Wahab, E. A., & Ratnasingan, M. (2013). Religiosity and fear of death: a three-nation comparison. Mental Health, Religion & Culture, 16(2), 179-199.

[48] Burpo, Todd (2010) Heaven is for Real: A Little Boy's Astounding Story of His Trip to Heaven and Back. Nashville: Thomas Nelson Publ.

[49] Blank, O., Ortigue, S., & Landis, T. (2002). Stimulating illusory own body experiences. Nature, 419, 269-270.

[50] "Heaven still waiting: Publisher pulls book after boy recants on visit to heaven." http://retractionwatch.com/2015/01/16/heaven-can-wait-publisher-pulls-book-boy-recants-visit-heaven/ (accessed August 13, 2019).

[51] Freudenrich, C. (2009). "What Are the Four Fundamental Forces of Nature?" http://science.howstuffworks.com/environmental/earth/geophysics/fundamental-forces-of-nature.htm (accessed August 13, 2019).

[52] "List of multinational festivals and holidays" http://en.wikipedia.org/wiki/List_of_winter_festivals (accessed August 13, 2019).

[53] "Festival of Lights" http://en.wikipedia.org/wiki/Festival_of_Lights_(disambiguation) (accessed August 13, 2019).

[54] "March equinox" http://en.wikipedia.org/wiki/March_equinox#Human_culture (accessed August 13, 2019).

[55] Lipka, M. (2014). "Attending a Seder is common practice for American Jews" https://www.pewresearch.org/fact-tank/2014/04/14/attending-a-seder-is-common-practice-for-american-jews/ (accessed August 13, 2019).

[56] "Religion in Sweden" http://en.wikipedia.org/wiki/Religion_in_Sweden (accessed August 13, 2019).

[57] "Expressing and embodying our feelings" (2006) Pan: the Magazine of World Pantheism http://www.pantheism.net/pan/free/pan18.pdf (accessed August 13, 2019).

[58] https://shj.org/ (accessed August 13, 2019).

[59] https://aeu.org/ (accessed August 13, 2019).

[60] http://oasis.org/ (accessed August 13, 2019).

[61] http://www.secularhumanism.org (accessed August 13, 2019).

[62] http://www.secularhumanism.org (accessed August 13, 2019).

[63] https://www.atheists.org/ (accessed August 13, 2019).

[64] https://ffrf.org/ (accessed August 13, 2019).

[65] https://secularstudents.org/ (accessed August 13, 2019).

[66] https://humanism.org.uk/ (accessed August 13, 2019).

[67] https://humanists.international/ (accessed August 13, 2019).

[68] http://www.pantheism.net (accessed August 13, 2019).

[69] https://www.naturalism.org/ (accessed August 13, 2019).

[70] Clark, T. (2008). http://centerfornaturalism.blogspot.com/2008/11/worldview-naturalism-in-nutshell.html (accessed August 13, 2019).

[71] Church of the Flying Spaghetti Monster www.venganza.org (accessed August 13, 2019).

[72] Tooley, M. (2015). "The Problem of Evil," The Stanford Encyclopedia of Philosophy (Spring 2019 Edition), Edward N. Zalta (ed.), https://plato.stanford.edu/archives/spr2019/entries/evil/ (accessed August 13, 2019).

[73] "Planetary habitability" http://en.wikipedia.org/wiki/Planetary_habitability#cite_note-NASA1-1 (accessed August 13 2019).

[74] "Extraterrestrial life: The Drake Equation" http://en.wikipedia.org/wiki/Extraterrestrial_life#The_Drake_equation (accessed August 13, 2019).

[75] Gott III, J. Ret, al, (2005). A map of the universe. The Astrophysical Journal, 624(2), 463.

[76] "Multiverse" http://en.wikipedia.org/wiki/Multiverse (accessed August 13, 2019).

[77] Tyson, N. (1998). "The Greatest Story Ever Told" https://www.haydenplanetarium.org/tyson/essays/1998-03-the-greatest-story-ever-told.php (accessed August, 13, 2019).

She holds a Diploma in Poetry Writing and is currently studying for a MA in Creative Writing. She is a poetry mentor for the Koestler Trust, a charity which helps ex-offenders with their creative practice. Her work has been published in a number of anthologies. Jacqueline also performs her poetry as part of theatre productions.

Jacqueline is available for workshops, readings and mentoring.

You can contact Jacqueline on:

Twitter: @jewelmarkpress

Email: jewelmark@hotmail.com

Website: www.jewelmarkpress.co.uk

www.ingramcontent.com/pod-product-compliance
Lightning Source LLC
Chambersburg PA
CBHW072040040426
42447CB00012BB/2952